Small Consolation

The Dubious Benefits of Small Business for Job Growth and Wages

Is Small Beautiful for Workers?

by Dale Belman and Erica L. Groshen

Small Business Employment Dynamics Revisited

by David W. Stevens and Julia Lane

Economic Policy Institute

1660 L Street, NW, Suite 1200, Washington, D.C. 20036
ISBN: 0-944826-67-9

DALE BELMAN is an associate professor of economics at the University of Wisconsin-Milwaukee.

ERICA L. GROSHEN is assistant vice president, Federal Reserve Bank of New York. At the time this study was written, she was an assistant professor of economics at Barnard College, Columbia University, New York.

JULIA LANE is an associate professor in the Department of Economics, The American University, Washington, D.C.

DAVID W. STEVENS is executive director of the Jacob France Center, University of Baltimore.

The two studies included in this report were completed in 1995. Anyone wishing to discuss the findings further may contact the authors directly at the following e-mail addresses:

Dale Belman • *drdale@csd.uwm.edu*
Julia Lane • *jilane@american.edu*
David W. Stevens • *dstevens@ubmail.ubalt.edu*

ECONOMIC POLICY INSTITUTE
1660 L Street, NW, Suite 1200
Washington, D.C. 20036

http://www.epinet.org

Library of Congress Catalog Card Number: 96-84467

ISBN: 0-944826-67-9

TABLE OF CONTENTS

EXECUTIVE SUMMARY

Small business has long enjoyed a favorable spot in the public imagination. It is often portrayed as the engine of economic growth in the U.S. economy and extolled as the source of economic virtues such as job growth, entrepreneurship, innovation, cost reduction, and flexibility. This favorable image has brought considerable rewards in terms of public policy, and laws are often written to partially or fully exempt small firms from oversight and regulation.

But what do small firms do for workers and the economy that other firms do not? Do they create more jobs relative to their size than do larger firms? Moreover, are the jobs they create good jobs, with any relative advantage in terms of wages, benefits, and security?

The two studies that make up this report find that, whatever the other economic merits of small firms, they generate about as many jobs for their size as do larger firms, and their employees are often worse off than workers in larger concerns, which tend to pay more and provide better benefits. This large-firm advantage is shared across all types of workers, industries, and countries, and it has persisted for more than a century.

An extensive review of previous literature and an examination of recent data show that:

- While new and expanding small businesses (those with fewer than 50 employees) create new jobs at a higher rate than their larger counterparts, they also eliminate jobs at a higher rate. Thus, with respect to net job creation, there is no apparent pattern with respect to business size.
- Employees of large firms – those with 1,000 or more employees – are substantially better compensated than employees of small firms, particularly those with fewer than 25 employees.
- Employees of large firms are more likely to receive pensions and medical insurance than are employees of small firms. Only 13.2% of employees in small firms are covered by pension plans, compared to 68.7% of larger-firm employees. Likewise, only 30.0% of employees in small firms have health insurance, compared to 78.4% of employees in large firms.
- Large firms provide greater job security. Average job tenure in large firms is 8.5 years, compared to only 4.4 years in firms with fewer than 25 employees.
- While it is true that part of the gap in compensation between employees of large and small firms is attributable to differences in education and mix of occupations, the benefits for workers in large firms and establishments remain substantial even after adjusting for these differences.

Whatever the other economic merits of small firms, they generate about as many jobs for their size as do larger firms, and their employees are often worse off than workers in larger concerns.

- Establishment size – the number of employees in a single location – is also important. After adjusting for education, occupation, and firm size, employees in establishments with 1,000 or more employees earn 17-21% more than employees in establishments with fewer than 25 employees.

A comprehensive answer to the question of why large employers pay more is not yet available. But in any case, large firms are doing well by employees, and themselves, by providing jobs with higher wages and benefits and greater job security. Public policy, rather than favoring small business by exempting it from many forms of regulation, should strive to be size neutral. It should also support efforts to better understand the sources of the superior employment conditions at large firms so that they can be spread throughout the economy.

PART I

Is Small Beautiful for Workers?

BY DALE BELMAN AND ERICA L. GROSHEN

The authors thank Reagan Murray and Kristen Monaco for superb assistance with their research and Dr. Edith Rasell for her guidance.

INTRODUCTION

Small firms have always had a favorable image. They are frequently portrayed as the engine of economic growth in the U.S. economy, and they are extolled as the source of economic virtues such as innovation, cost reduction, flexibility, job growth, and entrepreneurship. Larger companies are instructed to find prosperity in imitation of smaller firms' means and techniques.

The favorable image of small firms has translated into considerable influence on public policy, and, as a result, laws are often written to partially or fully exempt small firms from oversight and regulation. For example, firms with under $500,000 in revenue are not covered by minimum wage laws; the Family Medical Leave Act applies only to firms with 50 or more employees; the Toxic Substance Control Act of 1976 exempts small chemical companies from testing and reporting requirements; the Occupational Safety and Health Administration exempts firms with fewer than 20 employees from regular inspections; and the Office of Federal Contract Compliance exempts businesses with fewer than 50 employees from filing affirmative action plans. Even Securities and Exchange Commission reporting requirements are more stringent for larger firms.[1]

Yet, whatever the economic merits of small firms, their employees are often worse off than those in larger firms. An extensive literature documents that, for more than a century, large firms in every industry and every country have paid more and provided better benefits than have small firms.

Based on a review of the literature and an examination of recent data, we find:

Employees in large firms on average earn 39% more than employees in small firms.

- The employees of large firms (those with 1,000 or more employees) are substantially better compensated than employees in small firms, particularly those with fewer than 25 employees.

- Employees in large firms on average earn 39% more than employees in small firms.

- Employees in large firms are more likely to receive pensions and health insurance than are employees in small firms. Only 13.2% of employees in small firms are covered by pension plans, compared to 68.7% of employees in large firms. Only 30.0% of employees in small firms have health insurance coverage, compared to 78.4% of employees in large firms.

- Large firms provide greater job security. Average job tenure in large firms is 8.5 years, compared to only 4.4 years in firms with fewer than 25 employees.

- While it is true that part of the gap in compensation between employees of large and small firms is attributable to differences in education and mix of occupations, the gains to employment in large firms and establishments remain substantial even after adjusting for these differences. When workers with equal levels of education and occupational attainment are compared, employees in large firms earned on average 11.5% more than those in small firms. They also had a 43.4 percentage-point advantage in pension coverage, a 32.4 percentage-point advantage in health insurance coverage, and a 2.2-year job tenure advantage over employees in the smallest firms.

- Establishment size – the number of employees in a single location – is also important. After adjusting for education, occupation, and firm size, employees in establishments with 1,000 or more employees earn 17- 21% more than employees in establishments with fewer than 25 employees.

- It is not entirely clear why large employers pay more. Current research indicates that the higher wages and better benefits associated with large firms are not due solely to more highly skilled or better-trained employees, worse working conditions, or the sharing of monopoly profits. Part of the answer may lie in the economic efficiencies achieved by large firms.

This report summarizes the current understanding about the differential between employer size and wages and examines current data for the evidence on trends. We begin by summarizing the findings of previous research about the connection between wages and employer size. We then explore the explanations that have been advanced and the empirical evidence that supports or undermines those theories. We close with an examination of recent data to identify the latest trends and current magnitude of employer-size/employee-wage differentials.

EMPIRICAL EVIDENCE ON THE EFFECT OF EMPLOYER SIZE ON WAGES

Wages vary substantially among workers with identical skills and traits, and one of the most important sources of this variance is employer size. Despite differences in scope, data, and approach, virtually all studies of this phenomenon conclude that some employers pay more than others and that size is a central component of the difference (Groshen 1991b reviews this literature).

A comparison of the overall difference in wages and benefits between firms of different sizes is a useful starting place for analysis. However, such measures capture all differences in wages between large and small employers, whether they result from size per se or from other factors, such as an employee's education and occupation, that are correlated with employer size. The use of regression analysis to adjust for correlated factors is essential to obtaining accurate estimates of firm-size effects; variants on this technique are universal throughout the literature on this topic.

Table 1-1 summarizes a broad range of literature on the size–wage differential; it documents the existence, persistence, and characteristics of the phenomenon, as well as tests of models for the differential. These studies vary in their use of continuous or discrete measures of size, the inclusion of fringe benefits, industries covered, countries covered, and attention to disparities in impact on different types of workers. Data availability underlies many of the differences in approach, but the studies combine to form a coherent, albeit complex, picture: larger employers pay substantially higher wages than small employers, the effect of employer size on total compensation is greater than the effect on wages, the relationship between employer size and wages has existed through most of this century, and the relationship holds true in both developed and developing countries.

A Brown and Medoff (1989) study provides the most exhaustive investigation of the size–wage differential in the United States. Using virtually every data source with information on size of employer, the authors consistently find large size–wage differences – between 6% and 15% for the U.S. private sector.[2] They conclude that these differences are not readily explained by the various theories proposed by economists.

The Perlman (1940) study shows that employer-size effects have been apparent to social scientists for most of the 20th century. Schmidt and Zimmerman (1991), Schaffner (1993), and Blanchflower and Oswald (1990) provide evidence that the size–wage gap prevails internationally, in both industrial and developing countries with a wide range of labor market institutions.

Studies that focus on wages rather than total compensation may significantly

Virtually all studies in this area conclude that some employers pay more than others and that size is a central component of the difference.

7

TABLE 1-1
A sample of empirical studies of establishment- and firm-size–wage differentials

Authors and year	Data	Relevant conclusions
1. Perlman 1949	BLS Establishment Surveys; Wages and Hour Statistics for six industries	Hourly earnings are higher in large firms, within industry, occupation, product group, and region. Earnings are not affected by establishment size, holding constant region.
2. Lester 1967	BLS Industry Wage Survey and Census of Manufactures (1967)	Except for textiles, apparel, and aircraft, earnings increase with establishment size. Differentials increase when fringe benefits are included.
3. Masters 1969	BLS Census of Manufactures	Plant size variable is a larger and more significant determinant of average wage differences among industries than concentration.
4. Buckley 1979	BLS Area Wage Surveys for 29 areas	Controlling for industry mix, wages rise with area cost of living, but not with establishment size.
5. Miller 1981	BLS Census of Manufactures	Controlling for industry, wages increase with size of establishment.
6. Personick and Barsky 1982	BLS National Survey of Professional, Technical, and Clerical Pay 1980	Pay levels tend to increase with employer size, but above-average levels are associated only with large firms. Wage premia attributable to a firm's size are larger for entry-level than for experienced professional workers. Corporate size has better explanatory power for professionals, while establishment size does better for clerical workers.
7. Mellow 1982	Current Population Survey 1979	Both plant size and firm size are positively associated with wages, controlling for personal characteristics and concentration. The effect is proportionately larger when fringe benefits are included. Industry-plant size interactions were insignificant.
8. Brown and Medoff 1989	Wide variety of public sources	Firm and plant size are associated with higher wages, controlling for worker characteristics, occupation, industry, and working conditions. Even when wages are held constant, worker attachment is stronger at large employers. Within detailed professional, technical, and managerial occupations, employer size premia are smallest in the highest pay grades. The size premium exists even where there is no threat of unionization. The size–wage effect does not shrink much when you look at wage changes for workers who move to different-sized employers. Even piece rate workers receive a size–wage premium.
9. Dunn 1980, 1984	Independent surveys of employee wages, working conditions, and employer size within one industry	Large firms pay higher wages and shift premia than small firms, except in highest-paid occupations. Compensating differentials do not appear to be the cause, infers the presence of bargaining.
10. Groshen 1991a	BLS Industry Wage Surveys of production workers' wages in six manufacturing industries	Within detailed job classification, wage variation between establishments accounts for 30-60% of wage variation. Half of the differentials were associated with characteristics of the establishments (size, union affiliation, product, pay method, etc.).

TABLE 1-1 *(cont.)*
A sample of empirical studies of establishment- and firm-size–wage differentials

Authors and year	Data	Relevant conclusions
11. Groshen 1991b	BLS Area Wage Surveys of nonsupervisory workers' wages (blue collar and white collar) in one SMSA for six years	Within detailed job classification, wage variation among establishments accounts for 20-70% of wage variation. Differentials were stable over six years and not easily related to size changes.
12. Antos 1983	Employer Expenditure for Employee Compensation Survey (1977); Area Wage Surveys 1976-78; 1977 and 1979 Current Population Surveys	In aggregate, large firms pay both higher wages and more compensation to their employees. The firm size premium is much less for unionized workers than for nonunion workers. Relative to firms with fewer than 100 employees, workers in large, unionized firms experience 0.1% wage premium and 5.4% compensation premium, whereas workers in large nonunion firms receive a 10.6% earnings premium and a 14.8% compensation premium over small firm workers.
13. Garen 1985	1969 National Longitudinal Survey; 1967 Census of Manufactures	There is a positive association between firm size and wages and firm size and years of schooling. Young men from wealthier families are more likely to be employed at larger firms.
14. Barron, Black, and Loewenstein 1987	1982 Employment Opportunity Pilot project by the Center for Research in Vocational Education and followup survey	Larger employers screen more applicants prior to making an offer, are more likely to provide on-the-job training, and use more capital-intensive production processes than small firms. Larger firms pay higher starting wages, although the employer size–wage differential decreases for workers who have been employed for over two years.
15. Barth, Cordes, and Haber 1987	May 1979 Current Population Survey	Increased education raises probability of being employed at a large firm. Older workers are more likely to be employed in a small firm. Prior labor force experience increases likelihood of employment at a small firm. Women are more likely to find employment in a small firm than men.
16. Evans 1987	Small Business Database 1976-80	The probability of firm survival increases with size and age of firm. Firm growth decreases with size and age. Firm growth increases with the number of plants, holding firm size and age constant.
17. Miller 1987	1976 Annual Survey of Manufactures	Within detailed industry, large firms have 34% higher labor productivity (value added per hour worked) than small firms, which their 60% higher capital intensity (book value of fixed assets per production worker hour) cannot plausibly account for.
18. Evans and Leighton 1989	1981 National Longitudinal Survey of Young Men; 1983 Current Population Survey	Company size has a larger and more statistically significant effect on wages than does plant size. Small firm workers have a more unstable work history and lower human capital endowments. Tenure increases with firm and plant size. Probability of being employed by a large firm is independent of total labor market experience.
19. Idson 1989	1973 Quality of Employment Survey	Tenure is increased with establishment size. More promotions and overall internal mobility with greater size. Effects are stronger in nonunion than union sector.

TABLE 1-1 *(cont.)*
A sample of empirical studies of establishment- and firm-size–wage differentials

Authors and year	Data	Relevant conclusions
20. Blanchflower and Oswald 1990	Workplace Industrial Relations Survey, 1980, 1984; British Social Attitude Surveys 1983-86	The factors that influence white-collar pay are essentially the same as those that affect blue-collar pay, i.e., the size of the workplace (positively), the proportion of part-time and female employees (negatively).
21. Belman and Heywood 1990	1983 May Current Population Survey	Federal government behaves as a large establishment with regard to wages offered; federal workers are not, on average, paid higher wages than their private sector counterparts in large establishments.
22. Idson and Feaster 1990	1976, 1977 Census of Manufactures; 1977 Quality of Employment Survey	Selectivity or nonrandom assignment considerations act to reduce the wages gap between small and large firms, based on statistically unobservable characteristics.
23. Idson 1990	1977 Quality of Employment Survey	Significantly greater rigidity and regimentation of work at larger establishments, but controlling for this there is no difference in job satisfaction across establishment size.
24. Kostiuk 1990	Salary and bonuses reported for chief executive officers of 83 U.S. manufacturing firms 1969-81; financial information on companies and characteristics of executives; cross-section for 1980 and historical data for 1934-39	Size is more important for the incomes of executives than for other workers. Negative coefficient on average hourly wage ($1 increase in average hourly wage to workers results in almost 7% decrease of manager earnings); firm size is the dominant factor in setting level of compensation for management.
25. Davis and Haltiwanger 1991	Longitudinal Research Datafile (1963, 1967, 1972, 1977, 1982); Current Population Survey	Real hourly wages rose steadily for all plant sizes over the years 1963-86, but there was a much larger wage increase at larger plants. The most important characteristic explaining wage dispersion is plant size – about 40% of the wage differential can be attributed to plant size.
26. Holtmann and Idson 1991	1972-73 Quality of Employment Survey	Plant size has a significantly positive effect on the likelihood of training. Large employers are willing to invest in training for "riskier" employees.
27. Kruse 1991	1980 Survey of Job Characteristics	Negative coefficient on supervision (more supervision results in lower wages), but the establishment size coefficient is unchanged with the supervision coefficient; no support for the "shirking" theory. Inclusion of the working condition variables decreases the magnitude of the establishment size coefficient.
28. Mayo and Murray 1991	Employment Security Master Employer and ES202 files for state of Tennessee, 1986	Larger, older firms are less likely to fail. The measure of employment risk is highly significant and exerts a negative effect on wages after controlling for the independent effects of firm size and age. Once employment risk is controlled for, there is no independent size effect on wages.
29. Rebitzer and Robinson 1991	1983 May Current Population Survey	The plant size–wage differential is smaller for workers in secondary sector than the primary sector. Firm size effect on wages in primary jobs is largely due to the presence of multiple plants rather than to increases in the number employed at all plants.

10

TABLE 1-1 *(cont.)*

A sample of empirical studies of establishment- and firm-size–wage differentials

Authors and year	Data	Relevant conclusions
30. Schmidt and Zimmerman 1991	1978 random survey of employed individuals in Federal Republic of Germany and West Berlin	The mobility variable (number of jobs in the last five years) is insignificant in explaining the size–wage differential.
31. Even 1992	1973, 1977 Quality of Employment Survey	Workers in large firms and/or with greater on-the-job training are more likely to have parental leave policies at their workplace. There is a positive correlation between presence of parental leave policy and higher wages.
32. Montgomery, Shaw, and Benedict 1992	1983 Survey of Consumer Finance; 1982 Census of Business; 1982 Source Book: Statistics of Income	There is a negative tradeoff between pensions and wages. A firm's willingness to provide a pension plan increases with size and with the capital/labor ratio.
33. Schaffner 1993	Peruvian Living Standards Survey 1985-86	Larger Peruvian employers provide substantially better wages, benefits, working conditions, and job security, even after control for measurable differences among employees.
34. Troske 1994	Worker-Establishment Characteristic Database (1990 U.S. Census merged with LRD data) – all manufacturing	Larger plants employ workers and managers with higher observable measures of skill. When type and amount of capital in the plant is included in wage regressions, it wipes out the employer size–wage premium.

understate the premium associated with employer size. Mellow (1982), Dunn (1984), and Antos (1983) find that high-wage employers pay a larger fraction of total compensation in the form of fringe benefits than do small employers. Large firms are also more likely to offer pension plans (Montgomery et al. 1992) and benefits such as parental leave (Even 1992). These factors would tend to make the wage gap smaller than the total compensation gap between large and small employers.[3]

Public discussion and academic papers frequently gloss over whether employer size refers to size of establishments (i.e., worksites) or firms (which may be composed of multiple establishments). Most size–wage theories explain establishment-size differentials but say little about the large-firm wage premium, beyond observing that firm and establishment size are positively correlated. Although Brown and Medoff (1989) and Troske (1994) find that establishment-size effects are larger than firm-size effects, the two concepts of size have independent positive effects on wages. Given that both exist, the distinction remains crucial for policy and for many theories that propose to explain the size–wage gap.

Another theoretically important dimension to the concept of employer size is how it should be measured – by the number of employees, sales, capital stock, or number of establishments. The most common measure of size is number of employees at the site or firm. However, a recent study by Troske (1994) finds that establishment capital stock is more closely related to wages than is number of employees.

Many studies have also explored which kinds of workers are most affected by the size of their employer. These results are difficult to summarize, because the various datasets include different ranges of workers and divide them up differently. While studies uniformly agree that the wages of all workers rise as employer size grows, they disagree about which workers benefit most from employment in large firms. Troske (1994) finds that the wages of nonmanagerial workers are more strongly influenced by employer size than are the wages of managers. Brown and Medoff (1989) find a more complex pattern. Although employer-size effects are fairly constant for blue-collar, clerical, sales, and other nonmanagerial, nontechnical occupations, the effect weakens in the highest pay grades for professional, technical, and managerial occupations.

Studies disagree about which workers benefit most from employment in large firms.

To summarize, despite the range of data, definitions, samples, and specifications, the body of evidence supports the view that large employers pay higher wages than do small employers, and that this relationship has persisted over many decades. We turn next to efforts to explain this relationship.

REASONS EMPLOYER SIZE MATTERS FOR COMPENSATION

Why do large employers pay higher wages? As we shall see, this robust relationship poses a difficult and only partially solved puzzle for economists.

The solution to this puzzle is relevant to policies for improving wages and employment. If the higher wages of large employers serve only to counterbalance factors such as poorer working conditions or to reward superior skills and training, then there is little to be learned from large firms. If, however, workers at large firms are earning their higher wages through higher employee productivity, or if large employers are able to pay more because they do something better than small employers, then determining what these firms are doing and spreading those practices may provide large gains throughout the economy. Even if the explanation of the source of the large-firm advantage is not fully understood, policies that encourage the growth of employment among larger employers may still serve to help a labor force suffering from worsening terms of employment.

The solution to the puzzle of the size–wage differential is relevant to policies for improving wages and employment.

Why size should not affect wages

The elementary economic model of the labor market starts with the assumption of perfectly competitive product, capital, and labor markets. In this world, employers in the competitive labor market face a single market wage for each type of employee, and they can hire as many workers as they like at that wage. How does the employer determine whether to hire an additional employee? The employer compares the addition to output (productivity) expected from that employee to the market wage. If the value of the additional output exceeds the wage, it is worth bringing on an additional employee. The employer stops hiring when the wage is just equal to the productivity of the marginal employee – the last hire. The employer earns the largest profit possible by following this rule: efforts to pay other than the competitive wage cannot succeed, since the employer will either not be able to attract sufficient appropriately skilled workers (compensation set too low) or will earn insufficient profits (compensation set too high).

How do employers decide the number of employees to hire? So long as the contribution of new hires to output exceeds what they add to costs, the employer should hire more workers. As the number of workers in a worksite increases, the contribution of the last worker hired starts to decline. At the point where the value of the next worker's added production would dip below the wage rate faced by all firms, the plant stops hiring. In other words, the wage (which, from the employer's view, is fixed) determines the size of the firm (which adjusts to the wage). Other factors, such as industry, capital stock, technology, and managerial skill, also influence employer size, but, after allowing for such factors, causation runs from the wage to employer size, not the other way around.

Despite the compelling logic of this simple model, the empirical work summarized in Table 1-1 suggests that it is wrong. Large employers pay higher wages, which raises two crucial questions: (1) why do the large employers pay high wages? and (2) why don't small employers lose their employees to large firms, or why aren't large employers replaced by smaller low-wage competitors? Answers to these questions require a more sophisticated model.

Most theories of the employer-size/employee-wage differential answer the first question by arguing that workers in high-wage firms are more productive. This answer also addresses the second question, because employees are always paid their "marginal" value to the firm. However, productivity-driven wage differentials are usually thought to be associated with differences among individuals, not with employers' characteristics. An explanation of size–wage differentials as an outcome of productivity requires a systematic link between size and workers' productivity.

Without such linkage, the size differential can be explained only by forms of imperfect competition, such as product market monopoly. But such explanations are less appealing, since the size effect has been found across a variety of industries with different product market structures and has been shown to persist even after adjustments for imperfect competition.[4]

There are four possible explanations for the observed relationship between employer size and wages: compensating differentials; matching or sorting by worker ability; efficiency wages; and rent sharing.

There are four possible explanations for the observed relationship between employer size and wages: compensating differentials; matching or sorting by worker ability; efficiency wages; and rent sharing. Employers maximize profits in all four theories, but they diverge from the basic competitive story in other ways. The first two explanations relax the assumption of uniformity among employees or working conditions among large and small employers. Then, hourly wages may mismeasure either the workers' units of work (because workers in large firms produce more per hour because of their superior skill) or their compensation (because the wage omits nonpecuniary returns to employment associated with size). By contrast, the efficiency-wage and rent-sharing models assume imperfections or lack of competition in product or labor markets, since they imply the existence of job rationing or queues for high-wage employers. The remainder of this section introduces each of the four potential explanations in more detail and reviews the associated empirical evidence. **Table 1-2** provides a summary of these competing theories.[5]

14

TABLE 1-2
Theoretical sources of employer-size–wage differentials

Theory	Wage equation	Costly factor(s)	Source(s) of heterogeneity	Additional assumptions necessary for employer size–wage effects
Compensating differentials working conditions, fringe benefits, effort	$w = MP$	Mitigation of undesirable terms of employment	Management strategies or technologies	Large employers have less desirable terms of employment, uniformly across all or most occupations.
Sorting by ability human capital, innate differences, job matching	$w = MP$	Training; monitoring of workers' effort; turnover	Management strategies or technologies, and innate or acquired worker quality; quality of job match	Large employers have higher monitoring costs or more ability-sensitive technologies, so they have higher average quality of workers, or matches, consistently across most occupations.
Efficiency wages monitoring, turnover, market insulation, corporate consistency, morale, loyalty	$MP = f(w)$ $\rightarrow$ $w^* = MP^*$	Monitoring of workers' effort; turnover; design of internal wage structure; firm-specific training	Management strategies or technologies, corporate size	Large employers adopt high-wage strategies (or technology has a similar effect on the efficient wage) across all or most occupations, workers in most occupations develop firm-specific training.
Rent sharing insider/outsider, bargaining, rent capture	$w = w_m + f(\pi,$ workers' bargaining power)	Monitoring of workers and/or of management	Size of rents, workers' ability to capture rents, and managerial altruism	In large employers, rents are higher, or ability to capture rents is higher; rents are shared among most occupations.

Compensating differentials

One of the earliest explanations of the size–wage effect was that large employers paid a premium – a compensating differential – because they offered working conditions inferior to those of small employers (see Masters 1969). In other words, the very factors that make employees in large establishments more productive – the division and routinization of labor – may also make work unpleasant. Thus, large employers may have to pay a premium beyond the wage paid by small employers to attract and keep an adequate number of suitable employees.[6]

The theory of compensating differentials holds that, if employers provide different working conditions, then, all else equal, the employer who provides poorer conditions must raise wages to attract an adequate supply of labor. The difference in wages between employers ensures that workers are indifferent between working for the employer with better conditions and the one who provides worse conditions.[7]

Poor working conditions by themselves cannot explain size–wage effects.

Although there are many conditions of work that might require compensating differentials, few are closely associated with firm or establishment size. For example, working conditions such as physical exertion are specific to occupations and exist across firms of varying size. If employer-size premiums are to be explained by compensating differentials, the quality of working conditions must deteriorate with increasing size. There may be some conditions, bureaucratic personnel policies, or monotony of jobs that may affect all or most workers in large firms and establishments and may require payment of a compensating differential.

This still leaves the second question: how do large firms afford the higher wages? The very conditions that require payment of a compensating differential, such as division and routinization of labor, also increase the productivity of employees of large firms. This higher productivity pays for both the wage premium and possibly increased profits.

For researchers, the essence of the theory of compensating differentials may be one of mismeasurement. What has been called a premium to firm size is actually a payment to employees to induce them to put up with the bureaucratic and routinized nature of their employment. The challenge for researchers is to remove the effects of working conditions from the firm-size measure.

With the exception of differentials for risk of injury and death, there is little evidence that wages are influenced by working conditions (see, for example, Smith 1979 and Brown 1980).[8] Among the studies that consider employer size, Idson (1990) and Dunn (1980, 1984) find that controls for working conditions reduce the size–wage premium little, if at all, although Kruse (1991) finds somewhat larger effects. Medoff and Brown (1989), who include a number of measures of size-related factors such as second- or third-shift work, extent of choice in overtime hours, and dangerous or unhealthy situations and their severity, also find little effect on the size–wage premium.

There is little support for the central premise of the compensating differentials argument in the current literature. Of the working conditions examined by Brown and Medoff, only 21 of 42 showed a negative relationship with establishment size. Idson (1990) finds that large nonunion establishments offer their workers higher mobility (that is, more frequent promotions and job changes), and others (Even 1992; Barron et al. 1987; Holtmann and Idson 1993) find that the amount of employer-provided training rises with employer size. The strongest evidence that employees in large firms are less "satisfied" with their working conditions is found in Idson (1990), who reports that workers find jobs in large establishments more rigid and less satisfying. However, contrary to the theory, adjusting worker satisfaction for the size premium does not equalize worker satisfaction between different-sized employers.[9] Additional evidence that compensation is not equalized across

There is little support for the central premise of the compensating differentials argument in the current literature.

employer sizes is found in the reduced quit rates (Brown and Medoff 1989) and longer tenure (Evans and Leighton 1989) of those working for larger employers.

To summarize, the evidence leans strongly against efforts to explain size–wage effects as mismeasured payments for differentials in working conditions.

Human capital approaches: sorting by ability and matching

It is well established that the workforces of larger firms are older, are better educated, and have a higher level of education than the typical American worker (current data are provided in a subsequent section of this study). This raises two questions: first, why do large firms need a superior workforce, and, second, is the size–wage effect really a measure of the superior pay required by the superior workforce of large firms? As we shall discuss in detail, there are a variety of answers to the first question. The answer to the second question is less complex: current research finds that, even after adjusting for the productivity-enhancing characteristics of the labor force of large employers, the size premiums remain large and robust.

Human capital theory, formalized by Becker (1964) and Mincer (1974), explains the link between increased education and training on the one hand and wages on the other. Training increases the productivity of a trained person's time over that of the unskilled. However, the costs of training (such as tuition and forgone wages) constrain the supply of skilled workers. Thus, the price of trained labor is higher than that of untrained labor and reflects the difference in marginal product between the two.

If human capital differences are manifested as wage differences between employers, the employers must be able to predict productivity on the basis of acquired training (education and seniority), and both hire and pay workers accordingly. High-wage employers are such because they select the most able workers in each occupational category. Low-wage employers hire (or end up with) the least productive workers across the board.[10] (See Groshen 1991b for further discussion of this point.) There may also be productivity-related wage differences between employers if some aspects of productivity are innate – associated not with training but rather with traits such as individual motivation – and if employers are able to detect these traits and hire based on them.

Although the link between human capital and productivity is well accepted, conventional models of competitive firms do not provide an obvious explanation of why a large employer would choose to hire only high-ability employees. If all workers were paid their marginal products, the quality of workers paid to produce a certain product should be irrelevant. For example, employers should be indifferent between two equally productive workers at one wage and a single doubly pro-

Current research finds that, even after adjusting for the productivity-enhancing characteristics of the labor force of large employers, the size premiums remain large and robust.

17

ductive worker at twice the wage. Any worksite could have a distribution of productivity levels (all rewarded accordingly) within each occupation. In this world, no employer-size differentials would arise.[11]

For innate or acquired productivity differences to generate size–wage differentials, employers must choose workers of fairly uniform productivity within occupations and apply this policy similarly to all occupations. That is, this theory must explain why employers segregate and also why large employers choose high-productivity/high-wage workers while smaller employers choose the low-productivity/low-wage alternative.

Sorting or matching models start with the observation that large employers hire more-productive workers and pay accordingly and develop a consistent logic to explain this observed relationship.

The models that address this issue are referred to as sorting or matching models. These models of the size–wage premium start with the observation that large employers hire more-productive workers and pay accordingly and develop a consistent logic to explain this observed relationship. The source of differences in productivity between workers (worker heterogeneity) may be innate advantages (e.g., genetic or motivational) or acquired differences (e.g., education or work experience). In all versions, large and small employers earn zero or equal profits in equilibrium.

One story, introduced by Oi (1983), posits that size per se raises the per employee costs of managing because it stretches the limited resources of the top manager. Large employers economize on these costs, called monitoring costs in this literature, by hiring more-skilled managers and workers, who need less monitoring. The wages of managers and workers then rise with the number of employees in the plant or firm. Barron et al. (1987) extend this theory by arguing that large employers will choose a high-wage/stringent-screening recruitment strategy in order to attract the most highly qualified workers and deter poorly qualified applicants, hence economizing on subsequent monitoring costs.

An alternative to the monitoring-cost story is one that argues that employer technologies may be differentially sensitive to a worker's ability. One version of this approach argues that the technologies of large employers are more sensitive to employee skills than are the technologies of small employers, and that this difference attracts highly skilled employees (who must be paid high wages) to such firms. In this story, employees whose high potential is unrealized by a technology that is insensitive to their ability have an incentive to seek out a job where they can stand out and be paid accordingly. This motivation generates a positive correlation between the ability-sensitivity of the employer's technology and the average quality of its applicant pool. Thus, employers with ability-sensitive technologies hire disproportionately more high-ability workers and, therefore, pay higher wages.

How does this response to technology generate a relationship between employer size and wages? Dunne and Schmitz (1992) argue that large employers are more likely to choose skill-sensitive capital. They have to hire more-skilled workers and pay their higher wages. For example, enterprises using the most advanced production technologies must be operated by flexible, highly trained workers, whereas traditional labor-intensive production can be performed by minimally trained employees.

Alternatively, capital intensivity (capital per worker) or the total quantity of capital (both closely related to employer size) may create the need for high-productivity employees. Both suggest that capital and skill are complementary (Griliches 1969; Hamermesh 1980, 1983; Sattinger 1980) – in effect, the more capital a firm or establishment has, the more ability-sensitive it is.[12] For example, more complex, expensive capital may require more skill for efficient operation; the more capital surrounding the worker, the more can be ruined by mistakes or ineptitude; or settings with a wide variety of capital may require more flexibility and broader training in workers. If capital and skill are complements in production, capital and skilled labor work most cost efficiently together, while unskilled employees are most cost efficient in low-capital environments. In this story, capital intensity (capital per worker) proxies well for ability-sensitivity. As large employers tend to be capital intensive, wages will also be correlated with size.[13]

Large employers may also employ more-skilled labor and pay accordingly simply because they have larger capital stocks per se.

Large employers may also employ more-skilled labor and pay accordingly simply because they have larger capital stocks per se. Troske (1994) describes such a model, predicated on differences in managerial skills between large and small employers, and confirms the unsurprising correlation between establishment employment and capital stock, even within closely defined industries. Hence, the quantity of capital (rather than the type of capital or the number of employees) could determine the optimal quality – and wage – of workers hired.

A second technology-driven version of the sorting theory suggests that variation in the quality of workers in an establishment imposes negative externalities on the productivity of more-able workers (Akerlof 1981). Think of establishments as assembly lines where workstations are indivisible, or where the timing of the output depends on the speed of the slowest operative. Then, the productivity of the slowest worker determines the productivity of all the workers. As workers seek their best-paying job, establishments become segregated by quality. Employers maximize profits by hiring or retaining (through their recruitment and termination policies) only those workers at least as able as those in their existing workforce.[14] Job matching provides another variant on sorting models (Jovanovic 1979), one driven by unobserved traits. Here, both worker and employer are uninformed about the worker's productivity in a particular job until both have experienced it. Although the possible range of productivity of a worker – job combination is known, the productivity of a particular worker on a particular job is not known in advance and cannot be guessed from the worker's known skills. An employer's initial wage offer is based on the productivity of the average worker in the job, and workers accept jobs that pay more than their current jobs. Wages are then adjusted over time to reflect workers' actual productivity. As the accuracy of productivity measurement improves with tenure, the wages of employees with bad matches decline, and they eventually leave in hope of finding a better match elsewhere. Workers with good matches (i.e., high productivity) remain to enjoy their high wages.

How might this generate an employer-size premium? Differences in the distribution of productivity across employers would lead to sorting of employees and systematic differences in wages between employers. In particular, if large employers have productivity distributions of higher variance – perhaps because of externalities among workers, or more expensive or varied capital – then the matching model predicts higher wages for large employers in much the same way as do the ability-sensitivity models. In large firms, workers with the best matches stay for a long time, and workers with the worst matches leave quickly.[15]

The central difference between the matching-model and the ability-sensitivity story is simply that, in matching, workers and employers need to experience the match to learn its productivity – productivity is not predetermined by the worker's ability. In contrast, the typical sorting model simply assumes that employee productivity is known in advance, and the employer can choose the appropriate employee without difficulty. Matching theory suggests the important role of personnel departments in large firms – a large employer must be able to sort carefully among workers in search of these elusive traits. It also suggests that large employers effectively hire and retain a higher-quality labor force through their policies for recruitment, promotion, forced separation, and wage setting.

> **Evidence regarding traditional measures of human capital consistently shows that large employers tend to have more-educated, better-trained workers. However, such sorting accounts for at most half of the raw size–wage premium.**

Studies of how much of the size–wage premium can be explained by sorting vary in results.[16] Evidence regarding traditional measures of human capital consistently shows that such sorting is present: large employers tend to have more-educated, better-trained workers (see Masters 1969; Brown and Medoff 1989; Garen 1985; Barth et al. 1987; Troske 1994). However, such sorting accounts for at most half of the raw size–wage premium, leaving the 6-15% premium identified by Brown and Medoff unexplained.

An issue faced by researchers is that some productivity traits are not included in the datasets they use to investigate wages. Such issues are explicit in matching theory, which suggests that not even the parties directly involved are able to observe all relevant productivity traits. This problem is compounded by the typical dataset, which may not include productivity-related measures of characteristics such as health status or quality of education. This problem is lessened where innate qualities are correlated with the usual acquired human capital variables – such as education, age, and experience – as these variables also capture innate differences. Where there is no such correlation, economists can only control for unobserved productivity indirectly, an approach that leads to considerable imprecision and controversy over the interpretation of their results.

Tests for sorting and matching by unmeasured characteristics provide less support for these theories than does research using measured characteristics. Idson and Feaster's (1990) study of the 1979 May Current Population Survey suggests that sorting may actually run the other way – high-quality workers may sort to the unstructured environments of small firms. Evans and Leighton (1989) argue that unobserved heterogeneity may account for all or most of the size–wage premium in a small sample of full-time white men drawn from the National Longitudinal Survey. However, the low significance of the size–wage differential in that study is as much a product of small sample size as it is an outcome of controlling for unobserved characteristics. Brown and Medoff (1989) perform a parallel experiment, obtain similar results, and conclude that there is little support for the unobserved heterogeneity hypothesis.

More recently, Troske (1994) finds that including plant capital stock, plant investment (as a proxy for high-tech capital stock), and mean level of supervisory staff education in a wage regression effectively wipes out the effect of plant size on wages. Since capital seems to be more important than workforce size, these findings refute Oi's (1983) monitoring model. They support the ability-sensitivity/capital-skill complementarity hypothesis that large plants hire workers and managers with superior attributes that are observed by the firm but not by the economist. However, since this evidence is indirect, it fails to rule out many competing hypotheses. (In particular, Troske mentions that large firms may provide more in-house training, but job matching and many other possibilities still remain.) Alternatively, the research may simply indicate that capital stock, rather than number of employees, is the appropriate measure of establishment size.

These inconclusive results pose problems for the unmeasured-ability explanation for the size–wage effect. These theories also face the same hurdle that plagues the compensating differentials model: explaining the low quit rates and high tenure levels found in large firms, even controlling for wage level (Brown and Medoff 1989). If workers are sorted by ability among employers and paid accordingly, quit rates should be equalized across firms and plants. Lower quit rates for large employers suggest these jobs are rationed, unless high ability is strongly associated with employment stability. Garen's (1985) finding that, all else equal, young men from wealthier families are more likely to be employed at large firms also suggests that jobs in large firms may be rationed, unless being a male with wealthy parents signals higher unmeasured ability.

Idson and Feaster's study suggests that sorting may actually run the other way – high-quality workers may sort to the unstructured environments of small firms.

21

To summarize, sorting and matching theories both argue that the apparent relationship between establishment size and wages is actually measuring the greater use of high-productivity/high-wage employees by larger firms. However, research on this issue finds substantial employer-size premiums even after adjusting for observed human capital traits such as education, occupation, and job experience. Results with models that depend on unmeasured characteristics do not convincingly indicate that employer-size premiums simply proxy for worker ability.

Efficiency wages

The theory of efficiency wages was first developed to explain the existence of involuntary unemployment in competitive markets. It did this by positing that firms might want to pay a wage above the market rate to obtain high levels of productivity from their employees. In the context of this study, efficiency-wage theories are used to explain why large firms might gain an advantage by paying wages above those of smaller firms. Research on efficiency wages is not very advanced, but there is little indication that the employer-size premium is explained by factors associated with efficiency-wage schemes.

The theories of efficiency wages differ in that they posit a causal relationship between wage levels and a worker's on-the-job productivity.

Most theories of wages argue that increases in productivity cause increases in wages. The theories of efficiency wages differ in that they posit a *causal* relationship between wage levels and a worker's on-the-job productivity. A high wage induces workers to be more productive than they would be in a low-wage environment. Efficiency-wage employers pay workers a premium above the market-clearing wage because the resulting increment in productivity yields the highest profits. Employer-size versions of these theories assert that wage premiums raise productivity more in large firms than they do in small firms, and thus large firms are more likely to find it advantageous to pay efficiency wages. The increased productivity has been modeled as coming from three sources: reduced monitoring (or shirking) costs, decreased turnover, and sociological considerations. The internal labor market literature adds two explanations that are clearly size related: market insulation and corporate consistency.

In the monitoring/shirking version, workers' effort is costly to monitor (Bulow and Summers 1986; Shapiro and Stiglitz 1984). Higher wages reduce a worker's incentive to shirk, because shirking increases the probability of losing a high-wage job. In comparison to an employer paying the equilibrium wage, efficiency-wage employers pay higher wages, experience higher worker productivity, and have lower direct-monitoring expenses. If, as Oi (1983) and others suggest, large firms have higher monitoring costs because owners are more removed from operations, then they may be more likely to pay efficiency wages to reduce the need to monitor.

The turnover version emphasizes employer costs of hiring and training (Salop 1979). Wages above equilibrium reduce turnover because workers have fewer superior alternatives and/or because the general level of unemployment rises. Thus, workers paid higher wages have longer tenure. Two related search/recruiting versions of the model show that firms with high costs of unfilled vacancies may offer high wages to fill vacancies more quickly (Lang 1987; Montgomery 1987). Again, if larger employers have higher costs of hiring and training, then they would be more likely to use high wages to reduce turnover.

A third variant of the argument is based on sociological morale, loyalty, or teamwork effects. Group work norms are raised by wages above the minimum required (Akerlof 1982). Such devices may be more necessary in the impersonal setting of a large firm.

The two internal labor-market variants, as described by Doeringer and Piore (1971), focus on (1) the out-of-pocket and morale costs of designing a compensation package for a group of employees and (2) firm-specific human capital. Keeping wages set constantly to market-clearing levels requires periodic readjustments in response to shocks in the external labor market. Yet, redesign of wage schedules may be expensive for large employers. In addition, changes in relative wage relationships may be perceived as inequitable or as a breach of implicit contract, and may thus lower effort or raise turnover. An alternative to frequent, disruptive adjustments to market fluctuations is to pay above-market wages. If, on average, workers receive a premium, then wage shocks that are small relative to the premium will not force a firm to readjust its compensation package. Employers save out-of-pocket and productivity costs of the adjustment, at the expense of a higher wage bill.

Corporate consistency, the second internal labor-market version, is based on the tendency of firms to promote workers from within rather than hire from outside, presumably to retain workers with firm-specific human capital. Such a policy requires that internal wages for each occupation in each plant be no less than: (1) local wages for the occupation (or the workers will leave the firm), and (2) firm-wide wages for that occupation (or workers will refuse transfers within the plant). This implies identical wage structures for plants within the firm regardless of location, with each occupation earning the maximum local rate over all plant locations. On average, this yields wages that increase with the number of plants, but the theory would not predict a size–wage premium among single-establishment employers.

Efficiency-wage models explain the size–wage differential among firms by invoking economically important heterogeneity among employers of different sizes: differences in technology (for example, vintage effects) or in products (for example, differentiated quality niches). Workers paid the market-clearing wage queue for jobs at the elevated wage, while recipients of the high wage avoid job loss or

If larger employers have higher costs of hiring and training, then they would be more likely to use high wages to reduce turnover.

quitting because of the scarcity of equivalent opportunities. Efficiency-wage explanations of the size–wage gap also require that most occupations in the establishment are affected similarly. The plausibility of this assumption depends on the version of the model in question.

Interest in efficiency-wage models stems, in part, from their implications for employment policies. For example, as is implicit in sorting and matching models, if the reason that various demographic groups are less likely to be employed in, and earn the superior wages of, larger firms is that they are less productive, then interventions to redress the inequality should focus on eliminating human capital disparities. However, if the inequality stems from institutional barriers that deprive some workers of access to large-firm jobs paying efficiency premiums, then policy needs to focus on alleviating employment discrimination.

Most empirical studies that implicate efficiency wages or rent sharing as an explanation for inter-employer differentials rely heavily on the process of elimination of other theories and circumstantial evidence. These studies offer important, but necessarily indirect, evidence.[17] Few direct empirical tests of efficiency-wage models have been performed, primarily because of the lack of appropriate data. Their results have been mixed.

If workers' efficiency rises with their wages, then models of production that include measures of wages should find a positive relationship between wages and output. Miller (1987) finds that, controlling for industry, labor productivity is higher in large establishments. However, although Kruse (1991) finds that heavily supervised workers earn lower wages, inclusion of supervisory intensity does not reduce the establishment-size differential. Thus, the shirking hypothesis does not appear to explain the size–wage gap. In addition, Brown and Medoff (1989) note that no size–wage differential should be necessary for workers paid by piece rate, yet among piece-rate workers in BLS Industry Wage Surveys, the establishment-size/employee-wage differential appears even larger than among hourly rate workers. The researchers perform a number of other tests of implications of the monitoring version of the size–wage differential that yield little support for that variant of the theory.[18]

Efficiency-wage theories provide an interesting and potentially important explanation of the size–wage premium. The testing of the theory is in its early stages, and current work is inconclusive. Although the weight of evidence currently leans against the version of the theory that suggests efficiency wages are a substitute for monitoring, there is not sufficient evidence on other efficiency-wage models to support a conclusion. Further research will be required to establish if efficiency wages account for firm-size effects and, if so, which theory provides the best understanding.

> *Further research will be required to establish if efficiency wages account for firm-size effects and, if so, which theory provides the best understanding.*

Rent sharing

Another explanation for the size–wage differential is that large firms earn profits greater than those earned by typical firms and then share some portion of these so-called "economic rents" with their employees. Although there is evidence of a rent–wage relationship in other contexts, current research does not indicate that the size–wage differential is really a rent–wage differential.

When bargaining between workers and their employers takes place in the context of competitive labor and capital markets, bargained wages cannot differ from the market-clearing wage. Otherwise, the firm would close or the workers would leave. However, if an enterprise generates some economic rents (from imperfect competition or other sources), employees can lay claim to some of the rents generated by an enterprise through explicit or implicit bargaining with their employers. Wage settlements will then reflect both the size of rents and the balance of bargaining power of the parties. Thus, the existence of both rents to the firm and employee bargaining power are necessary conditions for wage bargaining to produce wage variation.

How might this generate the employer-size/employee-wage differential? One possibility is that large employers are more likely to earn and share unusually high profits (i.e., "rents") with employees in the form of higher wages. Alternatively, it may be that employees in large firms are in a stronger bargaining position relative to their employers, for a number of reasons: workers in large firms may know about whatever rents exist; training or hiring costs may be higher for jobs in large firms; employers may find that it is harder to ensure that employees at large work-sites do not sabotage or damage capital; or owners of large firms or plants may typically be further removed from day-to-day management, and so may not be able to detect any largess.

The models of a rent–size relationship differ in the identity of the bargaining agents and in the enforcement mechanisms for the bargaining. Most clear is the case of unionism, where the agents are the union and management. In a nonunion setting, the bargaining agent for the workers is not obvious. However, economists have long noted the existence of informal organization by workers in nonunion settings (Dunlop 1957). One version is the union-threat effect, where the threat of unionization forces owners to provide benefits similar to those the workers would receive if unionized (Dickens 1986). Since, all else equal, large workplaces are more vulnerable to unionization, this explanation has some appeal. Indeed, several patterns of the size–wage effect are consistent with the union-avoidance explanation: for example, the size–wage premium is larger in the nonunion sector and among production workers (Antos 1983; Brown and Medoff 1989). However, the existence of the size–wage effect in so many different countries, occupations, and industries, whether highly unionized or not, works against this explanation.

In the rent-sharing theory, large firms earn profits greater than those earned by typical firms and then share some portion of these so-called 'economic rents' with their employees.

25

Lindbeck and Snower (1987) outline versions based on firm-specific human capital. Since we have seen that larger firms provide more on-the-job training, employees of large firms may be in a stronger bargaining position than small-firm employees. This fact does, however, raise the question of why large firms persist in providing training.

In a another version of this model, referred to as agency-cost or managerial-capitalism models, managers mediate between labor and the owners of the firm. If management's compensation is poorly correlated with rents to the owners, or if managers care about worker satisfaction (whether through managerial altruism or as a result of the ability of workers to bring on-the-job problems to the fore), management may not maximize rents to owners. Implicit bargaining may occur, with management cast in various roles, from agent for the workers, to mediator between the two sets of interests, to agent for the owners. The latter role generates a model all but institutionally indistinguishable from a union-bargaining model.[19]

Current research does not support the theories of rent sharing.

Bargaining models lend themselves to the prediction of employer differentials with the addition of some assumptions that bind together workers of different occupations. At least three possibilities exist: (1) workers' bargaining power may be consistent across occupations; (2) workers may need to form large groups in order to exert bargaining power; or (3) managerial altruism may extend uniformly across occupations. If none of these seem plausible for all occupations, particularly between blue-collar and white-collar jobs, then more theory or another explanation may be needed.

As an explanation for size–wage differentials, bargaining models find little direct empirical support. Since the existence of rents rests on imperfect competition in the product market, a sizable portion of variation in rents should be associated with industry. In fact, as Brown and Medoff and others show, almost all of the size–wage effect occurs within industries. While some portion of the industry–wage differential may be due to rent sharing, the size–wage differential is hard to pin on this source.[20]

Within industries, Brown and Medoff find that large establishments have more elastic demand (implying that they have less latitude for raising prices without losing sales) than do small establishments, which contradicts the rent-sharing story. Although they do estimate that multi-establishment companies face less elastic demand than single-plant firms (as predicted), the effect is so small that it could have little impact on wages.

In summary, current research does not support the theories of rent sharing. However, the research on this topic is limited and is focused on the preconditions for rent sharing rather than on direct tests of the proposition. More carefully focused work may support different conclusions.

An integrated model

Another model, which combines elements of efficiency-wage, matching/sorting, and compensating differential theories, builds on the observation that large firms are both less likely to fail than small firms and provide greater opportunities for employees to move up within the organization (Idson 1995). Both factors increase employee tenure in the firm, thus making it profitable for firms to raise productivity through increased on-the-job training (OJT). This larger investment in employees encourages firms to take additional steps to retain their employees and so protect their investments. They screen for employees who are less likely to quit, and they implement compensation policies, such as paying above-market wages and providing pensions, to induce employees to remain with the firm. In this model, the high wages of large firms are a result of the greater efficiency of their labor forces, but the underlying cause of the efficiency and higher wages is the increased job tenure associated with the job stability and job opportunities provided by large firms.

Idson's theory is complex and, although evidence is generally favorable, not all aspects have been confirmed. Working with several datasets, Idson finds corroboratory evidence that larger firms provide greater opportunities for internal advancement, that voluntary quit rates are lower in larger firms, that firm failure rates reduce employee tenure, that larger establishments provide higher levels of OJT, that increased OJT is associated with increased tenure, and that longer tenure in large firms is closely related to the higher wages and benefits provided by those firms. However, the statistical relationship between increased internal mobility, OJT, and reduced turnover is weak. Even so, the majority of evidence is favorable, and this should encourage more research on these topics.

The integrated model builds on the observation that large firms are both less likely to fail than small firms and provide greater opportunities for employees to move up within the organization.

Conclusion

In keeping with Brown and Medoff (1989), this review of the literature finds that, although the evidence that large firms and establishments provide better wages, fringe benefits, and job security is overwhelming, a complete explanation of why this is so does not yet exist.

Researchers have put forward four theories to explain these effects: compensating differentials, rents, sorting/matching, and efficiency wages. Current research does not support the first two theories. The theory of compensating differentials finds no support, despite a substantial number of studies, as there is no evidence that employer size is a proxy for poorer working conditions. Indeed, much of the empirical evidence contradicts the initial assumption that working conditions deteriorate with increases in employer size. The negative evidence on rent sharing is thinner, as there are fewer studies and the tests of the theory are indirect.

The theories of sorting related to observable human capital characteristics find considerable empirical support; observable human capital characteristics account for one-third to somewhat less than half of the size–wage effect. Current literature does not find unobserved ability to be an important source of the size–wage relationship. Yet, there is some evidence suggesting that large firms may be able to use human capital more effectively because of their greater job stability and opportunities for internal mobility. Finally, there are relatively few tests of efficiency-wage models, and what tests there are provide varied results; confirmation will require additional research.

As explanations related to poorer working conditions of large employers (compensating differentials) or better employees (human capital) have either been eliminated or accounted for, the eventual explanation is likely to find that large employers' higher wages are derived from superior practices – but the nature of these practices is not yet clear. Whatever the final explanation, there is little doubt that large employers provide better jobs.

RECENT CHANGES IN SIZE–WAGE EFFECTS AND THEIR IMPLICATIONS

Evidence of a positive relationship between firm size and wages goes back more than 50 years. Although explanations for this correlation remain uncertain, its existence has not, until recently, been in doubt. The rapid evolution of the U.S. economy over the last decade has brought with it changes that may have weakened the advantages of employees of large firms. Large firms have been subject to increased competitive pressures, and they have been provided new opportunities for reducing labor costs. Some have responded by reducing employment and compensation and by diminishing the job security for those who survive. In contrast, small firms seem to have benefited from the economic climate of the 1980s and 1990s. For example, it is often argued that all of the current growth in jobs is taking place among smaller firms.[21] Given the difference in the economic circumstances of large and small firms over the past decade, it is reasonable to ask whether large firms are *currently* better employers – that is, providers of superior wages, hours, and working conditions – or, to be less extreme, whether the gap between small and large firms is diminishing. This is the topic of the balance of this inquiry.

Are large firms currently better employers, or is the gap between small and large firms diminishing?

We address this two-part question – whether a gap remains and whether it is shrinking – by first examining how different-sized firms compensated employees in 1993 and in 1979. The first section of the investigation uses data from the 1993 Benefits Supplement of the Current Population Survey (CPS) to depict the distribution of employment, wages, pension and health insurance coverage, job tenure, educational attainment, age, race, and sex by size of firms. The second section provides an analogous portrait for 1979, based on the 1979 CPS Benefits Supplement. This is compared and contrasted with the 1993 characteristics.

The third section provides a closer examination of the effects of firm size on wages, benefit coverage, and job longevity for 1993 and 1979. Building on the theories covered in the previous section, regression techniques are applied to the 1993 data to estimate the relationship between firm size and wages. Starting with a simplified equation, we add successive sets of controls for the determinants underlying the size–compensation relationship. We find that, although the controls reduce the magnitude of the measured relationship between firm size and the wage, it remains large and statistically significant. We then use the most sophisticated equation from this set to estimate a model for the 1979 wage data and for models for pension coverage, health insurance coverage, and job tenure for both 1993 and 1979. In the last section, this work is extended by narrowing the investigation to specific demographic groups, industries, and occupations.

We find no evidence that the effects of firm and establishment size are diminishing: in fact, the estimated effect of firm and establishment size on the wage was no smaller in 1993 than in 1979. We also find that, even after controlling for labor force demographics and other factors known to affect compensation, large firms continue to provide more generous pensions and health insurance coverage than do smaller firms and that, in keeping with the literature, the workforces of larger employers are older and better educated, and they have achieved higher occupational attainment, than those of smaller employers.

Our work does not support the view that size–wage effects are actually mismeasured compensating differentials. We also find that, although adjusting for the effects of sorting by observable human capital reduces the magnitude of the employer-size effects, large wage premiums for firm and establishment size remain. Evidence on the theory of rents is more complex. We find no evidence that larger employers voluntarily distribute industry rents in the form of higher wages. However, unionization allows employees to capture some rents, and this ability diminishes, but does not eliminate, employer-size effects. As with most research, our evidence on efficiency-wage theories is indirect and, therefore, somewhat inconclusive. To summarize, our research finds that larger firms and establishments continue to pay better wages and fringe benefits and provide more stable jobs, but, in keeping with other research on this topic, the explanation for the large-employer/better-job relationship remains elusive.

The economics and demographics of firm size: 1993

What proportion of employees are employed in the largest-sized firms? In the smallest-sized firms? How do large and small firms differ in pay, hours of work, or the educational attainment of their employees? Economic and demographic data from the 1993 Employee Benefits Supplement are presented in **Table 1-3**. The sample on which this study is based includes all individuals age 16-75 who report being employed in the private sector. The self-employed, a small proportion of the labor force, are not included. Firms are organized into five size categories according to whether they have fewer than 25 employees, 25-99 employees, 100-499 employees, 500-999 employees, or 1,000 or more employees.[22] Although the threshold for classification in the largest size category is well below the employment level of many large employers in the United States, it is sufficiently high to illustrate the difference between large and small employers.

Column 1 of Table 1-3 shows the distribution of employment by firm size in 1993 and illustrates the bipolar distribution of employment between large and very small firms: 40.8% of the labor force is employed by the largest-sized firms, 26.1% by the smallest firms. The next two smallest size categories, firms with 25-99 and

TABLE 1-3

Descriptive statistics on firm size, 1993

Economic characteristics

Firm size (employment)	% of total employment	Average wage	% employed in company that has some pension	% of employees covered by pension	% employed in company that offers health insurance	% of employees covered by health insurance	Tenure on current job	Average weekly hours
< 25	26.1	$ 9.39	18.5	13.2	41.6	29.9	4.4	35.8
25-99	14.0	$ 11.02	46.7	33.6	78.3	58.3	5.5	39.3
100-499	14.0	$ 11.92	72.1	52.9	91.4	72.2	6.3	40.2
500-999	5.1	$ 11.78	76.1	52.3	93.8	75.0	6.8	39.8
1,000 or more	40.8	$ 13.05	90.1	68.7	95.2	78.4	8.5	39.5

Demographic characteristics

Firm size	Average age	% female	% Black	% less than high school	% high school	% college	% graduate	% professional
< 25	36.2	48.4	6.5	37.4	25.9	20.5	16.2	28.5
25-99	36.8	45.2	5.5	15.7	13.9	14.2	9.7	14.6
100-499	37.3	48.0	6.0	12.6	13.7	15.3	19.6	10.0
500-999	37.4	48.4	9.4	5.0	4.2	4.2	4.5	8.8
1,000 or more	37.4	46.0	9.7	29.2	41.2	45.8	50.0	38.3

Note: Between 1979 and 1993 the U.S. Census shifted from reporting years of education as the highest grade completed to reporting degrees attained. As a result, the data on educational achievement is reported in somewhat different forms in Tables 1-3 and 1-4.

Source: Authors' analysis of Current Population Survey, Benefits Supplement, May 1979 and April 1993.

100-499 employees, together employ as many as the smallest category, while barely 5% of the labor force is employed by firms with 500-999 employees. Rearranging our data slightly, we find that firms with fewer than 100 employees and those with more than 1,000 employees account for 80% of the employed labor force, while only 20% work for firms with 100-999 employees.

Our data indicate the continued existence of a relationship between firm size and compensation. Turning first to wages, in 1993 the employees in the smallest firms earned an average wage of $9.39, while those in the largest firms earned $13.05, 139% of the wage of the smallest firms. The employees in the intermediate size categories had an average wage between $11.00 and $12.00, or 117-127% of the average wage of the smallest firms.

The 1993 CPS also provides data on the coverage of employees by pension and health insurance benefits. We consider two questions for each type of benefit: (1) did the company provide benefits for any company employee, and (2) did the reporting individual participate in the company plan? Pension plans included both defined-benefit and defined-contribution plans and company-sponsored individual savings account packages such as thrift, savings, and stock-option plans.[23] The effect of firm size on the coverage by pension and health insurance benefits is more pronounced than the difference in wages. While 90% of respondents in large companies report that there is a pension plan for some employees, respondents in companies of 500-999 and 100-499 employees answer that plans are less common. Moreover, fewer than half of respondents in companies with 25-99 employees and fewer than one-fifth of respondents working for small companies report there is a pension plan. Participation in the pension plan follows a similar pattern: close to 70% participation in the largest-sized firms, just over 50% participation in firms of 100-999 employees, about one-third of employees in firms with 25-99 employees, and only 13% in the smallest companies.

A similar although less extreme pattern is apparent for health insurance. Health insurance is always more common than pension plans regardless of firm size. However, employees of firms with fewer than 100 employees are noticeably less likely than those employed by firms with 100 employees or more to have any form of employer-provided health insurance. Over 90% of employees in firms with 100 or more report the firm has some form of health insurance, compared to 78% in firms with 25-99 employees and 42% in the smallest firms. Employee participation in plans shows a similar break: 72-78% participation in firms of 100 or more, compared to 30-58% in firms with fewer than 100 employees.

Job tenure, the number of years an employee has worked for his or her current employer, is an important dimension of job security. Here again, we find that, despite downsizing by some large employers, employee tenure remains longer in

The effect of firm size on the coverage by pension and health insurance benefits is more pronounced than the difference in wages.

larger firms. Those in the largest size category average 8.5 years with their employers, but this declines to only 4.4 years of service in the smallest firms.

Another dimension of job quality is whether an employer provides full-time employment. There is considerable concern over the adequacy of the jobs being generated by the U.S. economy, and one factor motivating this concern is the rise of part-time employment. Our research indicates that the smallest firms are the primary employers of part-time workers. Using average hours as a gauge, we find that employees in firms with fewer that 25 employees average 35.8 hours, while those in all other size classes average between 39 and 40 hours of work per week. A further breakdown of weekly employee hours indicates that half of employees working fewer than 20 hours per week and 37% of those working 20-34 hours are employed by firms with fewer than 25 employees.

As for demographics, the differences between firms of different sizes with regard to age, sex, and race are small. Age increases somewhat with firm size, from 36.2 years in the smallest-sized firms to 37.4 years in the largest, but the range, 1.2 years, is not large. Similarly, women are slightly more likely to be found in the smallest than in the largest firms – 48.4% compared to 46.0% – but again the differences are small. A slightly stronger pattern emerges with regard to race: African Americans make up almost 10% of the labor force of the largest-sized firms but only 5.5-6.5% of the labor force of the three smallest size categories.

Educational attainment varies more by firm size than do other demographic characteristics. If all firms had a similar demand for various levels of education, the proportion of variously educated workers would mimic the overall distribution of employment by size of firm. This is not the case. Workers with relatively low levels of education (those with less than a high school degree) are substantially overrepresented in the smallest firms and underrepresented in the largest firms. The proportion of the high school educated mimics the distribution of employment by firm size, but the college educated and those with graduate degrees are underrepresented in smaller firms and overrepresented in larger firms. The most notable deviation in this pattern is for employees with professional degrees, a group that is slightly overrepresented in small firms and slightly underrepresented in larger firms. This may reflect a tendency for some professionals to work in small partnerships or on their own with some support staff. This exception aside, the overall pattern is clear: small firms provide jobs for less-educated employees, while large firms provide the bulk of jobs for those with a college education and beyond.

The differences between firms of different sizes with regard to age, sex, and race are small.

The economics and demographics of firm size: comparison with 1979

Have the characteristics of different-sized firms changed over time? To answer this question we develop descriptive statistics by firm size from the 1979 Employee Benefits Survey (**Table 1-4**) and compare these with the 1993 characteristics discussed above.

In terms of the distribution of employment by firm size (column 1), the data show a striking shift in employment toward larger-sized firms between 1979 and 1993. Large firms accounted for 36.9% of employment in 1979; that share had risen to 40.8% by 1993. This shift was almost perfectly balanced by the decline in the proportion of employees in the smallest size class: from 31.0% to 26.1%. The proportion of employment accounted for by firms in the middle size categories remained virtually unchanged. This movement toward larger-sized firms runs counter to the perception that large firms are downsizing, but it comports with the renewed expansion of chain retailers and their effect on small employers in retail. (It may also be that the largest firm-size category – 1,000 or more – includes too many relatively smaller firms to capture the effects of downsizing among the largest firms in the country.)

What has happened to wages and benefits? To facilitate comparison, we have used the CPI-U-X1 to convert the 1979 hourly wage figures into 1993 dollars. Two trends are apparent in the data: first, the real wages of employees in firms with 100 or more employees have declined 5-8% since 1979; second, wages of employees in firms with fewer than 100 employees have remained virtually unchanged over this 14-year interval. These trends combined to reduce the gap between the wages offered by large and small firms. Firms of 1,000 or more paid 152% of the smallest firms wages in 1979, compared to 139% in 1993. For firms of 500-999 the premium fell from 133% to 125%, and for firms of 100-499 it declined from 131% to 125%. This pattern – wages declining in the largest firms and remaining stable in small firms – provides initial evidence that the firm-size/employee-wage relationship may have weakened under the impact of economic forces.

Additional evidence of the weakening of the relationship between firm size and compensation is apparent in the pension data. Although there is virtually no change in the size distribution of firms offering a pension plan to some employees between 1979 and 1993, there is a substantial decline in the proportion of employees participating in pension plans in the larger firms. Participation falls from 76.3% to 68.7% for firms with 1,000 or more employees, from 61.7% to 52.3% for firms with 500-999 employees, and from 44.4% to 33.6% for firms with 25-99 employees. Parallel to the wage findings, larger firms have reduced their provision of pensions, while smaller firms show little change from their low initial levels of participation.

The data show a striking shift in employment toward larger-sized firms between 1979 and 1993.

34

TABLE 1-4
Descriptive statistics on firm size, 1979

Economic characteristics

Firm size (employment)	% of total employment	Average wage	% employed in company that has some pension	% of employees covered by pension	% employed in company that offers health insurance	% of employees covered by health insurance	Tenure on current job	Average weekly hours
< 25	31.0	$9.35	18.3	12.8	31.8	n.a.	4.1	35.2
25-99	14.7	10.97	46.5	44.4	64.6	n.a.	5.1	38.9
100-499	12.6	12.22	69.1	53.2	76.9	n.a.	5.9	40.2
500-999	4.8	12.42	81.0	61.7	81.4	n.a.	6.4	38.9
1,000 or more	36.9	14.22	89.7	76.3	87.1	n.a.	8.7	40.1

Demographic characteristics

	Average age	% female	% black	Average years of school
< 25	34.8	48.1	7.1	11.8
25-99	36.2	42.7	6.2	12.0
100-499	35.7	43.6	6.6	12.4
500-999	35.1	47.6	5.5	12.7
1,000 or more	36.5	36.1	6.7	12.7

Source: Authors' analysis of Current Population Survey, Benefits Supplement, May 1979 and April 1993.

Our comparisons of health insurance coverage are restricted, since the 1979 survey asked only whether firms had health insurance for any employees. Contrary to trends in wages and pensions, each firm size showed an increase – between 8 and 14 percentage points – in the proportion with some health insurance plan between 1979 and 1993. The largest percentage-point increases occurred among firms with 25-99 and with 100-499 employees. Although larger firms remain more likely to have some form of health insurance than smaller firms in both 1979 and 1993, the gap has narrowed.

The distribution of job tenure and average hours changed little between 1979 and 1993. Although large firms increased their advantage in average tenure, the increase is small. Similarly, hours worked in 1979 and 1993 are similar: employees of the smallest firms continue to have a shorter average workweek, while other size categories average between 39 and 40 hours per week.

Finally, turning to demographics, average age increased across all sizes of firms. The smallest firms had the lowest average age, and the largest firms the highest average age. The increase in average age makes the decline in pension coverage more startling as, all else equal, increasing average age would be expected to be associated with increased pension coverage. Another notable change has been the increase in the proportion of women and African American employees in the largest-sized firms. The proportion of women in the labor force of the largest firms rose from 36.1% in 1979 to 46.0% in 1993. Similarly, the proportion of African Americans has risen from 6.7% to 9.7%. There is no evidence of similar patterns of change in smaller-sized firms.

Another notable change has been the increase in the proportion of women and African American employees in the largest-sized firms.

Firm-size effects on wages: controlling for coincident factors

To this point we have described only the relationship between firm size and compensation and working conditions. We have not formed an *estimate* that isolates the effect of firm size from other, potentially correlated, factors. For example, one variant on the sorting hypothesis predicts that large firms use their resources to find superior employees. If this is true, then at least part of the superior wage paid by firms that use such employees reflects those employees' superior abilities, rather than firm size. The theories reviewed earlier suggest a number of factors whose effects on wages need to be separated in order to measure the relationship between firm size and wages.

We begin our investigation with the simplest and most naive regression model of the relationship between firm size and wages: one that includes only firm-size measures among the explanatory variables. We then successively add factors that various theories suggest are the source of the relationship between firm size and wages. We find that the addition of controls for establishment size, human capital, demographic characteristics, and industry reduces the measured effect of firm size, but that the relationship between firm size and the wage remains economically meaningful.

We began by examining data for 1993. In the first model (the naive model with only firm-size measures as explanatory variables: **Table 1-5**, column 1), we find that firms with 25-99 employees pay approximately 17% more than firms in the smallest size category (1-24 employees) and that the premium continues to rise with employer size. Firms with 1,000 or more employees pay 38.5% more than do the smallest firms.

Although much of the discussion of employer-size effects is uncertain about the distinction between firm and establishment size, our next step is to distinguish the two by the addition of controls for size of establishment. Following the categories in the 1993 CPS, establishments are classified according to whether they have fewer than 10, 10-24, 25-49, 50-99, 100-249, or 250 or more employees. The smallest establishments provide the base of comparison. Turning to column 2, the addition of establishment controls reduces and flattens the measured firm-size effect but indicates very large wage premiums associated with establishment size. Firm-size effects vary between 10% and 15%; the largest firms and firms with 25-99 employees have the largest wage premiums, about 15%. Estimates of the establishment-size effects follow a more conventional pattern, with larger establishments paying more than smaller ones. The largest pay a premium of 39.6%; establishments of 100-249 employees pay a premium of 13.6%; and those with 50-99 employees pay an 8.3% premium. The combination of firm and establishment effects can produce very large premium: an employee of a firm that employs 1,000 or more and who works at a site with 250 or more employees would receive a 54.8% higher wage than a similar employee in the smallest-sized firm. Our conclusions follow those of Brown and Medoff (1989): establishment size matters more than firm size, but firm size is still important.

The theories of sorting and matching suggest that the apparent relationship between firm size and wages may be founded on a relationship between the skills of employees and wages. Our next two models address this hypothesis by successively adding controls first for educational attainment and age and second for occupation. Both sets of controls reduce the measured premium paid by mid-sized firms, but they have a more modest effect on the largest size categories. For example, for firms with 25-99 employees, addition of controls for educational attainment and age reduce the premium from 15.4% to 11.4%; further controls for occupation reduce the premium to 8.4%. In contrast, the premium for the largest-sized firm declines from 15.2% to 12.4%. The addition of these controls also reduces the

Firms with 25-99 employees pay approximately 17% more than firms in the smallest size category, and the premium continues to rise with employer size.

TABLE 1-5
Estimates of firm-size effects, 1993

	Only firm size	plus establishment	plus human capital	plus occupation	plus demographics	plus industry	plus unionization
Firm size							
25-99	17.1***	15.4***	11.4***	8.4***	5.9***	4.2***	5.9***
100-499	28.5***	13.9***	9.4***	7.2***	5.3***	3.5***	4.8***
500-999	31.4***	10.2***	7.9***	5.6**	3.8**	3.3*	2.6*
1,000 or more	38.5***	15.2***	13.2***	12.4***	11.6***	11.1***	8.2***
Establishment size							
10-24		3.6***	3.2***	4.1***	2.4**	2.8***	1.9**
25-49		-0.6	3.2*	3.3**	2.8*	3.6***	1.1
50-99		8.3***	9.0***	7.0***	5.9***	6.3***	3.6***
100-249		13.6***	13.6***	9.5***	9.3***	8.5***	6.8***
250+		39.6***	31.1***	22.5***	21.3***	17.7***	17.8***

*   Significant in a 10% test against a null of no effect
**   Significant in a 5% test against the null.
*** Significant in a 1% test against the null.

Note: Human capital variables include controls for educational achievement and age. Demographic variables include controls for race, sex, and region of residence.

Source: Authors' analysis of Current Population Survey, Benefits Supplement, May 1979 and April 1993.

premium associated with establishment size: the largest-size-establishment premium falls from 39.6% to 31.1% to 22.5%. Although the effect of these additions is to reduce the magnitude of the size–wage premium, it also restores the relationship in which the largest firms pay considerably more than smaller firms. Although our results provide support for sorting and matching theories, they also indicate that sorting and matching are not a comprehensive explanation of the size premium.

Although they are not strictly tied to any of the theories discussed in this paper, it has long been established that race, sex, and region influence wages. Our fifth equation adds controls for these factors to determine if they are related to firm- and establishment-size effects. With their addition, the premium paid by the largest-size firm declines slightly, to 11.6%, while that for the three other size classes becomes relatively uniform, between 3.8% and 5.9%. Establishment-size effects remain larger than firm-size effects: the largest-sized establishment pays a premium of 21.3%, the next largest 9.3%, the next below that 5.9%.

Our sixth equation adds controls for the major industry in which an individual is employed. These serve the dual purpose of removing the effects of compensating differentials and industry rents, both of which may be sources of the relationship between firm and establishment size and wages. As in our previous equations, the wage premium declines, but firm size remains a substantial determinant of wages.

The largest-sized firms pay an 11.1% premium, and the remaining three firm sizes pay a premium of 3.3% to 4.2%. The effect of establishment size also declines but remains large, particularly for the largest size categories: the largest-sized establishments pay a 17.7% premium, the next largest an 8.5% premium. There is then little evidence that industry rents account for the firm-size/employee-wage premium. The finding for establishment size is more favorable to the industry rents theory, although it is puzzling to find establishment rents unaccompanied by firm rents.

Our final set of equations considers the effect of bargaining power on the size effects. The mere existence of industry rents may not be sufficient to increase wages; workers may have to compel the sharing of rents through bargaining organizations. To control for the effects of bargaining, we drop our industry dummies and add two measures of unionization: individual membership and union density (the percent of employees in each industry belonging to a union).[24] The addition of these controls reduces the premium paid by the largest-sized firms to 8.2%. The coefficients on the other size categories range from 2.6% (500-999) to 5.9% (25-99). The premium associated with establishment size also falls for all but the largest size category. There is virtually no premium for establishments with fewer than 50 employees; establishments with 50-99 employees pay a 3.6% premium; those with 100-249 employees pay a 6.8% premium; and those with 250 or more employees pay a 17.8% premium. These results indicate that part of the firm- and establishment-size effects are union-bargaining effects possibly associated with the capture of industry rents or with union-associated productivity gains.

Nevertheless, substantial firm- and establishment-size effects remain. Even with controls for human capital, occupation, demographics, and union rents, an employee in the largest-sized firm and establishment would earn 26% more than an employee in the smallest firm.

To summarize, the addition of controls for employee skills, employee characteristics, and industry effects reduce our estimate of the premium paid employees of large firms and establishments, but the effect remains substantial. Without such controls, employees in large establishments have an estimated premium of 39.6%; employees of the largest-sized firms a premium of 15.2%. Once a full set of controls are included, employees in the largest-sized firms earn a premium of 11.1%, while employees in the largest-sized establishments earn a premium of 17.7%. Although there is little difference in the premium for intermediate-sized firms, it ranges from 3.3 to 4.2%; premiums for intermediate-sized establishments range from 2.8% for establishments with 10-24 employees to 8.5% for establishments with 100-249 employees. As of 1993, there is still a strong and substantial relationship between both firm and establishment size and wages, a relationship not fully explained by coincident influences.

The addition of controls for employee skills, employee characteristics, and industry effects reduce our estimate of the premium paid employees of large firms and establishments, but the effect remains substantial.

TABLE 1-6
Estimates of firm-size effects: wages, hours, and benefit coverage, 1979

	Wages[a]	Job tenure	Company offers pension plan	Individual participates in pension plan	Company offers health plan
Firm size					
1-24	–	–	57.9	45.7	66.7
25-99	-5.6***	-1.4	44.0***	34.0	62.2***
100-499	-1.9**	0.1	45.7***	43.0***	65.3
500-999	- 0.9	-1.2	54.7***	44.6	65.2
1,000 or more	9.1***	2.4***	75.9***	61.1***	73.4***
Establishment size					
25-100	7.4***	2.5			
100 and larger	11.7***	4.6**			

* Significant in a 10% test against a null of no effect
** Significant in a 5% test against the null.
*** Significant in a 1% test against the null.

[a] Specification of the wage equation follows that of the industry equation reported in column 5 of Table 1-5.

Source: Authors' analysis of Current Population Survey, Benefits Supplement, May 1979 and April 1993.

Trends in measured size–wage effects: 1979-93

Has the effect of firm and establishment size changed since 1979? The comparison above of descriptive statistics on wages for 1979 and 1993 found the advantages to employment in large firms declining over this period. However, these statistics cannot distinguish changes in firm-size effects from those caused by shifts in coincident factors. We again turn to *estimating* firm- and establishment-size effects with regression techniques, using the counterpart of the equation in Table 1-5 that includes controls for human capital, occupation, demographic characteristics, and industry. Although changes in the Employee Benefits Supplement between 1979 and 1993 preclude use of identical specifications for equations spanning these years, the equations are generally comparable and provide the most precise means of determining how firm-size effects have changed over time.[25]

Table 1-6, column 1, reports estimates of the employer-size premium for 1979 (the 1993 counterparts are found in the sixth column of Table 1-5). The wage premium paid by the largest-sized firms in 1979 is strikingly similar to that found in 1993: 11.1% in 1993 and 9.1% in 1979. The results for the intermediate size categories is the reverse of those anticipated from the descriptive statistics. In 1979, firms with 500-999 employees paid no more than the smallest firms, and those with 25-99 and 100-499 employees paid 1.9-5.6% less than the smallest firms. By 1993 these firms paid 3.3-4.2% more than the smallest firms. Establishment-size

TABLE 1-7
Estimates of firm-size effects: wages, hours, and benefits coverage, 1993

	Tenure	Company offers pension plan	Individual participates in pension plan	Company offers health plan	Individual participates in health plan
Firm size					
1-24	–	62.4	20.5	50.1	41.2
25-99	0.334*	46.7***	39.1***	83.2***	63.9***
100-499	0.64***	62.1	49.4***	88.7***	66.9***
500-999	0.77***	52.6***	50.5***	91.3***	71.0***
1,000 or more	2.2***	83.1***	63.9***	93.9***	73.6***

* Significant in a 10% test against a null of no effect
** Significant in a 5% test against the null.
*** Significant in a 1% test against the null.

Source: Authors' analysis of Current Population Survey, Benefits Supplement, May 1979 and April 1993.

premiums appear to have been stable over this period. Establishments with 25-100 employees paid a premium of 7.4% in 1979, somewhat above that paid by similar sized establishments in 1993. Establishments with 100 or more employees paid an 11.7% premium in 1979; by 1993 the premium paid by establishments with 100-249 employees was 8.5%, and for establishments with 250 or more employees it was 17.7%. The decline in the average wage of employees in large firms reported in the descriptive statistics is thus attributable to shifts in the distribution of education and occupational and industrial attachment between size categories. Thus, these estimates suggest that firm- and establishment-size premiums have remained constant or have increased since 1979.

Benefit-coverage premiums: 1979-93

As with wages, we are interested in isolating the effects of firm and establishment size on benefit coverage and job security and in determining how this effect has changed between 1979 and 1993. Although regression techniques are inappropriate to qualitative data, a closely allied technique termed Probit can be used to the same end. Again, we use our most sophisticated specification, one which includes controls for human capital, occupation, demographics, and industry, to isolate the effects of firm and establishment size from those of coincident factors. We turn to a discussion of the 1993 estimates and then to a comparison with the results from 1979.

Estimates of the effect of firm size on benefit coverage and job security for 1993 are found in **Table 1-7**; those for 1979 appear in Table 1-6. Beginning with estimates of pension effects, we find that in 1993 large firms were more likely to have a pension plan than smaller firms, and individuals in large firms are substantially more likely to participate in the pension system. By these estimates, 62.4% of small firms have some form of pension plan. Although the intermediate categories of firm sizes are no more likely to offer a pension plan, 83.1% of firms of 1,000 or more employees do so. The effect of firm size on individual participation is much stronger: only 20.5% of employees in the smallest-sized firms participate in pension plans. Participation increases steadily with firm size, with the largest-sized firms having the highest level of participation, 63.9%.

The 1979 data also show contrasts between the largest and smallest firms both in terms of pension plan availability and participation. However, participation was far less strongly tied to firm size in 1979 than in 1993. With the exception of the largest firms, there was little relationship between firm size and participation in 1979: 45.7% of employees in the smallest firms are predicted to be covered by pensions in 1979; firms with 25-99 and 500-999 employees have statistically indistinguishable rates of employee participation; and firms with 100-499 employees have a 2.7-percentage-point lower rate of participation. The largest firms have a 61.1% participation rate, 15.4 percentage points higher than the smallest firms. By 1993 employee participation in pension plans was 43.4 percentage points higher in the largest firms than in the smallest firms. Even the intermediate categories show substantially higher participation in 1993: participation is 18.6 percentage points higher in firms with 25-99 employees than in the smallest category and nearly 30 percentage points higher for firms with 100-499 and 500-999 employees.

Whether the company offers some health plan, and whether the reporting individual participates in a health insurance plan, is also strongly related to firm size. Again, including controls for employee skills, occupation, demographics, and industry affiliation, we find that in 1993 large firms were, by 43.8 percentage points, more likely to offer some health plan, and employees were, by 32.4 percentage points, more likely to participate in health insurance than employees in the smallest-sized firms. Even employees in the second-smallest size category were better off, more likely by 22.7 percentage points to be covered by health insurance than were employees in the smallest-sized firms.

Comparison to the 1979 data presents sharp contrasts. Again, we only have information on whether the firm offered some health insurance in 1979. Still, we find that, while employees report that firms with 25 or more employees are more likely to offer health insurance in 1993 than in 1979, coverage by the smallest size category has fallen from 66.7% to 50.1%. In contrast, the proportion of employees reporting that the largest-sized companies offer health insurance has risen from 73.4% to 93.9%.

Finally, there has been little change in the relationship between job tenure with the current employer and firm size between 1979 and 1993. Using the "industry" equation to estimate the size–tenure relationship, we find that in 1993 employ-

Health insurance coverage by the smallest size category has fallen from 66.7% to 50.1%.

42

TABLE 1-8
Descriptive statistics on firm size, 1993

Distribution of occupations

Firm size (employment)	Percent of total	Managerial & Professional	Sales	Clerical	Service	Craft	Operative
< 25	26.1	20.3	27.1	24.5	32.8	31.5	17.4
25-99	14.0	14.4	12.8	13.7	15.5	14.9	14.3
100-499	14.0	16.7	11.3	13.2	13.4	12.2	17.8
500-999	5.1	6.2	3.3	5.6	4.1	4.2	15.7
1000 or more	40.1	42.4	45.6	43.0	34.6	37.2	45.2

Distribution of employment by industry

	Construction	Manufacturing	Transportation	Communication & utility	Trade	FIRE*	Service	Professional	Medical
< 25	54.6	8.8	16.8	6.1	28.5	20.6	45.5	41.0	19.7
25-99	20.8	11.8	16.8	11.4	15.2	12.3	12.5	18.1	13.2
100-499	12.9	16.5	9.6	7.8	10.9	14.9	12.7	15.9	17.9
500-999	0.3	7.4	4.7	4.3	4.0	3.9	3.4	4.1	9.9
1000 or more	11.4	55.5	55.7	70.3	41.4	48.2	25.9	20.9	39.3

* Finance, insurance, and real estate.

Source: Authors' analysis of Current Population Survey, Benefits Supplement, May 1979 and April 1993.

ees in the largest firms had approximately 2.2 years more tenure than employees in the smallest firms; in 1979 this difference was estimated to be 2.4 years. Intermediate-sized firms had no job tenure advantage in 1979, but by 1993 there was a small but positive relationship between job tenure and firm size.

Overall, the estimates for pensions, health insurance, and job tenure complement those for wages: there is a strong relationship between firm size and firms offering pensions and health insurance, between firm size and employees covered by pensions and health insurance, and between firm size and employee tenure. Furthermore, the relationship between firm size and benefits is becoming stronger over time as small firms reduce their provision of benefits.

Firm-size effects by demographic group, industry, and occupation

To this point our analysis has taken in the entire economy; we now turn to specific demographic groups, occupations, and industries. There are considerable differences in distribution of firm sizes by occupation and industry (**Table 1-8**). By occupation, we find that small firms use relatively few managerial and professional employees (20.3%) and operatives (17.4%). In contrast, they account for a large share of the employment of service and craft employees. The largest firms em-

43

TABLE 1-9
Estimates of firm/establishment-size effects, by occupation

	Blue collar	White collar	Service
Firm size			
25-99	8.6***	12.2***	0.3
100-499	12.9***	10.8***	-4.2
500-999	13.2***	10.0***	-2.7
1000+	28.5***	15.5***	3.7
Establishment size			
10-24	2.5	-3.5***	-3.5***
25-49	-2.2	-4.7***	-4.9**
50-99	-0.8	-1.6	-6.1***
100-249	-4.1***	1.1	4.7*
250+	4.8***	9.4***	10.8***

* Significant in a 10% test against a null of no effect.
** Significant in a 5% test against the null.
*** Significant in a 1% test against the null.

Source: Authors' analysis of Current Population Survey, Benefits Supplement, May 1979 and April 1993.

ployed more than a proportionate number of sales and clerical workers and operatives, while accounting for relatively few service and craft employees. As noted in our discussion of descriptive statistics, there is little difference in the distribution of employees by race and sex across different-sized firms, although African American employees compose a larger portion of the labor force of larger firms.

There are similar differences in the distribution of firm sizes by industry. The largest-sized firms are particularly common in manufacturing, transportation, communications and utilities, and, to a lesser extent, finance, insurance, and real estate (FIRE); they are less common in construction, other services, and professional services. The reverse holds true for smaller firms: they are particularly common in construction, other service industries, and professional services, but they are underrepresented in health services, FIRE, communications, transportation, and manufacturing. In contrast to all other industries, the distribution of employment in wholesale and retail trade is similar to that of the full economy.

The specification of the wage equations used for occupation- and industry-specific equations follows that used for previous wage models. All include controls for education and age, individual characteristics, region, and establishment size. Industry equations include controls for occupation, and occupation equations include industry controls. As the occupations used to define our equations – white collar, blue collar, and service – are broad, these equations incorporate controls for less-aggregate occupations.

Firm-size effects differ substantially between occupations (see **Table 1-9**). There

TABLE 1-10
Estimates of firm/establishment-size effects, by industry

	Manufacturing	Construction	Trade	Other services	Professional services
Firm size					
25-99	6.2**	16.8***	2.0	8.1**	9.6
100-499	1.4***	29.1***	1.3	3.5	3.7***
500-999	6.4**	60.0***	-5.8***	2.8	7.7***
1000 or more	26.3*	26.4***	2.9***	5.5*	9.4***
Establishment size					
10-24	2.0	8.2**	-5.7***	-4.1	-7.4***
25-49	-0.3	-2.3	-5.2***	-1.9	-3.2
50-99	-2.6	-1.6	1.4	-4.1	-6.4***
100-249	-3.5**	-8.9**	-2.5	2.6	6.3***
250or more	4.8***	5.6	10.6***	3.6	12.2***

* Significant in a 10% test against a null of no effect.
** Significant in a 5% test against the null.
*** Significant in a 1% test against the null.

Source: Authors' analysis of Current Population Survey, Benefits Supplement, May 1979 and April 1993.

are large firm-size effects for blue-collar employees, somewhat smaller effects for white-collar employees, but none for service occupations. The wage premium paid blue-collar workers in the largest-sized firm, 28.5%, and the premium paid similarly situated white-collar workers, 15.5%, are substantially larger than the 11.1% premium estimated in the equations for all occupations (see Table 1-5). Premiums for blue-collar workers increase steadily with firm size, from 8.6% in firms of 25-99 employees to 13.2% in firms of 500-999 employees. The premiums for white-collar workers show much less variation, ranging from 10.0% to 12.2% for intermediate-sized establishments. Our estimates indicate no firm-size effects for service employees.

In contrast to the firm-size effects, occupation-specific establishment-size effects are smaller and more varied than those for all occupations. Blue-collar, white-collar, and service employees in the largest establishments receive a wage premium, the size of which is inversely related to the premium paid for firm size. The smallest premium in the largest establishments goes to blue-collar employees (4.8%), the next smallest to white-collar employees (9.4%), and the largest (10.8%) to the group that had no firm-size premium, service employees. There is little established pattern of premiums for intermediate-sized establishments; the only positive outside the largest establishments is the 4.7% premium paid to service occupations in establishments of 100-249 employees.

There are also considerable differences in firm- and establishment-size effects by industry (**Table 1-10**). Again, the largest firms all pay a wage premium, but the size varies greatly by industry. The largest, around 26%, are found in manufacturing and construction. In contrast, wholesale and retail trade have a 2.9% premium, other service industries pay a modest 5.5% premium, and professional services pay a 9.4% premium. The effects of firm size are strong in manufacturing, construction, and professional services, but the premiums do not always increase with firm size. Construction has a particularly large premium, 60%, for firms with 500-999 employees. In contrast, the effects of firm size are weak in other services; only half of the coefficients are statistically significant, and the premium for firms with 25-99 employees is larger than that for firms of 1,000 or more.

As we found for occupations, establishment-size effects are weaker in industry-specific equations than in equations for the full economy. The premiums paid by the largest establishments can be large in some industries – 10.6% in trade and 12.2% in the professional services – but several industries (construction and other services) pay no premiums for even the largest establishments. While the lack of conventional establishment-size effects in construction may be due to problems defining establishment for construction employees, this is not the case for service industries. Again, the pattern of effects in establishments with fewer than 250 employees is mixed, with positive, negative, and nonsignificant coefficients.

The results for different industries may help solve the discrepancy in the apparent weakening that appeared in our descriptive statistics in the firm-size/wage relationship between 1979 and 1993 and the strengthening of that relationship that we found in the regression estimates. The industries that have the weakest size–wage relationship, trade and service, are also the industries that have grown most rapidly in the 1980s. In contrast, the industries with the largest size–wage effects have either grown slowly or have lost employment over this same period. The movement toward a smaller size–wage relationship in the descriptive statistics reflects the shift in the distribution of employment toward industries with weak size effects rather than an attenuation of size effects themselves.

Turning to our final issue, we estimate equations for African American men, African American women, white men, and white women (**Table 1-11**).[26] Again, we use an equation with controls for human capital, occupation, demographic characteristics, and industry affiliation. We find that the magnitude of the firm-size premium varies considerably by race and sex, but all equations indicate that a substantial premium is paid to all employees in the largest firms and to almost all employees in the largest establishments. Males, African American and white, receive a 21-22% premium for employment in the largest-sized firms. Women of either race receive a 13% premium when employed in the largest firms. White men and women also receive premiums when employed in intermediate-sized firms – around 13% for men and 6% for women – while African Americans do not. White men and all women, but not African American men, receive a wage premium when employed in the largest establishments.

African American and white males receive a 21-22% premium for employment in the largest-sized firms. Women of either race receive a 13% premium when employed in the largest firms.

TABLE 1-11
Estimates of firm/establishment-size effects, by demographic group

	White male	Black male	White female	Black female
Firm size				
25-99	13.3***	1.7	5.9***	3.3
100-499	13.3***	-0.5	5.8***	0.0
500-999	12.9***	4.6	6.4***	-14.0
1,000 or more	21.0***	21.9***	13.0***	12.9***
Establishment size				
10-24	0.0	2.9	-3.6***	-9.5**
25-49	-3.8***	-12.9***	-4.8***	2.5
50-99	-1.5	4.0	-3.8***	-5.6
100-250	-1.8	1.6	1.8	3.0
250+	7.5***	5.6	10.0***	10.9***

*   significant in a 10% test against a null of no effect
**   significant in a 5% test against the null.
*** significant in a 1% test against the null.

Source: Authors' analysis of Current Population Survey, Benefits Supplement, May 1979 and April 1993.

To summarize, we find that firm-size effects vary substantially by occupation, industry, and demographic group. They are large in some occupations, both blue collar and white collar, and in some industries – manufacturing, construction, and professional services. They are notably attenuated in service occupations and other service and trade industries. We also find that establishment-size premiums are far more varied when disaggregated by industry and occupation than when estimated for the economy as a whole. Nevertheless, even with disaggregation by occupation and industry, we find that the largest firms and largest establishments pay a substantially higher wage than do smaller employers. Our demographic estimates reveal similar patterns in the data. Premiums for intermediate-sized firms and establishments show considerable variation; all demographic groups receive large wage premiums when employed by large firms, and most receive substantial premiums when employed in large establishments.

CONCLUSION

Although the positive relationship between firm size and employee compensation has endured for many decades, the steady drumbeat of favorable publicity for smaller firms prompts the question of whether employees of larger firms remain better off economically. Our review of 1993 data indicates that employees in large firms remain substantially better off with regard to wages, benefits, and job security. Furthermore, comparison to 1979 data indicates a widening rather than declining gap between large- and small-firm compensation.

Employees in large firms remain substantially better off with regard to wages, benefits, and job security than employees in small firms.

What do the literature and our current research allow us to say about the sources of these firm-size effects? It is useful to summarize the results. First, there is no evidence that firm- and establishment-size effects are a historic fluke that will fade over time. Firm-size effects have persisted, even through periods of increased competition such as the 1980s and 1990s. Second, firm-size effects are not just a "proxy" for compensating differentials. There is no evidence linking compensating differentials to employer-size effects, and there is considerable evidence that the premise of this literature, that large employers provide poorer conditions, is erroneous. Third, although there is evidence that human capital characteristics account for part of the employer-size effect, there is no evidence that employer-size effects are *only* a result of larger firms recruiting individuals with "better" human capital. All studies find that the addition of human capital variables and controls for occupation reduces measured employer-size effects. Prior literature and this study find that such factors fail to explain substantial firm- and establishment-size effects. Indeed, increased utilization of human capital may be an outcome of firm size and the job stability that accompanies such size. Fourth, although the literature indicates that size effects are not related to industry rents, we find evidence of size–rent effects in large establishments, perhaps partially explained by union bargaining power. However, even with adjustments for relationship between employer size and industry rents, there is still a strong independent relationship between firm and establishment size and wages.

What might explain the substantial balance of the effect? Following Brown and Medoff, we might conclude that, although we know larger employers offer better jobs, we cannot be sure why. Alternatively, it might be argued that efficiency wages provide the best remaining explanation. In this view, large firms and establishments use higher wages and benefits to obtain better performance from their employees. If this is the case, it may be possible to implement these policies at small firms, and such a step may offer a means of improving jobs without diminishing the economic performance of smaller employers. Although this proposal suggests important possibilities for policy, the evidence for efficiency wages may be viewed as too thin a straw to support major policy initiatives.

48

It may also be the case, as Idson suggests, that large firms can make better use of human capital (because the jobs they offer are more stable and they offer more internal mobility), so they are more willing to invest in their workers' human capital. If further research confirms this hypothesis, then the policies that encourage job stability and support firms that provide stable long-term employment could prove an important key to improving compensation. Indeed, such policies could be an essential complement to current efforts to encourage firms to bolster employee training.

Despite the lack of a simple explanation of the firm-size effect, it is clear that something that is good for workers, and their employers, is happening in large firms. From this perspective, any public policy advantage awarded to small firms (such as labor or environmental standard exemptions) should provide cause for worry.

While the issue of the relative quality of jobs in large and small employers has been resolved, this resolution raises another, more subtle issue. Small firms are often praised for their economic performance with little regard for the working conditions they offer. Our estimates suggest that the praise for small firms might be more circumspect if evaluators paid more heed to job quality.

To carry the point further, the results reviewed here indicate that the average small firm gains some competitive advantage (relative to the average large firm) from the low pay, inferior benefits, and reduced job security it offers employees. However, the pervasiveness of the size–wage differential across countries, industries, and time suggests that, for most large firms, any advantages of matching the low-wage strategy are dominated by important benefits derived from paying higher wages. The various theories we have explored all offer explanations for why large firms maximize profits by taking a high-wage strategy. Thus, large employers offer better terms of employment because they must, in order to maximize profits; small firms take the opposite strategy for the same reason. This implies that any argument that larger firms should emulate their smaller rivals' personnel policies is not only an argument for worsening the conditions under which Americans labor, it is also pointless – since it is not in the best interests of large employers.

The study of the relationship between firm size and employment conditions is far from complete. Perhaps more detailed study of firm-size effects by industry and occupation may help explain the source of firm- and establishment-size effects. Likewise, it would be useful to know about the relationship between firm size and benefit costs. Although much research remains to be done, clearly larger firms and establishments pay more, provide better benefits, and offer better job security. Small may be beautiful in many arenas, but it is not beautiful for workers.

Small may be beautiful in many arenas, but it is not beautiful for workers.

49

ENDNOTES

1.   See Brown, Hamilton, and Medoff (1990, 82-7) for a more complete listing and discussion of the exemption of small firms from federal regulation.

2.   "...an employee working at a location with ln(employment) one standard deviation above average can be expected to earn 6-15% more than a similar employee at a location with ln (employment) below average" (Brown and Medoff 1989).

3.   Similarly, Freeman (1981), Smith and Ehrenberg (1981), and Atrostic (1983) find that the inclusion of fringe benefits magnifies many types of wage differences among employers, not just the size–wage gap.

4.   Indeed, in the discipline within economics that studies firm behavior, some argue that the measured effect of imperfect competition on wages is largely a size–wage effect.

5.   The first column displays the four theories and their variants. Each source is developed from the competitive model by the introduction of transaction costs or nonuniformity among employees. The second column shows the wage equation implied by each theory. The third column lists the costly factors associated with the theories, and the fourth column presents the crucial assumed differences between large and small employers. The final column lists the theories' implied relationships and additional assumptions necessary for the models to predict the existence of apparent size–wage differentials (rather than differentials among individuals or among occupations).

6.   The theory of compensating differentials was described by Adam Smith in 1776 and is summarized in Smith (1979).

7.   This holds if worker tastes are identical. Otherwise, the differential depends on the tastes of the marginal worker.

8.   For unsuccessful investigations of working conditions as an explanation of industry wage differentials, see Krueger and Summers (1987) and Murphy and Topel (1987); for layoff risk, see Topel (1984).

9.   Since satisfaction is an inherently slippery concept to measure, this result is difficult to interpret, but it does not lend strong support to the compensating differentials story.

10.   Firm-specific human capital (Oi 1962) could also generate wage differentials within occupations. However, one would not expect this kind of human capital to lead to employer wage differentials because workers trade lower earnings in earlier years in return for higher wages later (see Groshen 1991b) for further discussion).

11.   In fact, among employers with similar output levels, this approach would yield a negative size–wage premium since the largest firms would employ the least productive workers, on average.

12.   Strictly speaking (see Sattinger 1980), capital-skill complementarity characterizes the adjustments to changes in the price of capital by a firm or economy with a fixed production function. If capital and skill are complements, a fall in the price of capital will raise the ratio of skilled to unskilled labor used. Sattinger (1980) coins the term "scale-of-resources" effect for the response of firms with different production functions to common factor prices. If capital-skill complementarity explains the size–wage differential, it is because large employers have access to cheaper capital and choose their capital and workers' skill level accordingly. If the scale-of-resources effect explains the size–wage differential, it is because large employers' production functions have different technologies (ones with more capital per worker) than their smaller counterparts have. Troske's (1994) model follows in scale-of-resources tradition by allowing managerial ability to enter the production function in multiplicative form.

13   This has been established only within the manufacturing sector. Miller (1987) shows it between and within industries; Idson and Feaster (1990) look at different measures without controlling for industry.

14.   Kremer and Maskin (1994) develop a more general treatment of when such segregation would occur.

15.   That is, workers with good matches in a company with high variance in productivity distributions earn considerably more than they would elsewhere, so they are unlikely to move, while those with bad matches in the same company earn considerably less, so they leave quickly. Thus, if the productivity distributions of large employers have higher variance than those of small employers, mean wages for large employers would tend to be higher than those for small employers.

16.   Many empirical studies suggest that other kinds of employer wage differences are not solely the product of sorting by measured human capital or by ability correlated with human capital. For example, Groshen (1989) finds that detailed occupation controls well for age, education, and experience, and that size–wage effects are large after control for detailed occupation. Dickens and Katz (1987a), Krueger and Summers (1988), and Murphy and Topel (1987) also reject sorting by usual measures of human capital as an explanation for inter-industry differentials.

17.   See Groshen (1991b) for a summary of a number of tests of the efficiency-wage hypothesis in general.

18.   Interest in these models suggests that the results of other tests may be available shortly. These tests will have to overcome the problem of disentangling substitution effects (the predicted tradeoffs) from scale effects (e.g., firms with high demand for effort both pay a higher wage and supervise heavily). Furthermore, investigators will need to devise ways and data to distinguish between efficiency premiums and close alternative explanations, for example, compensating differentials for effort, or human capital premiums for low propensity to quit, or shared rents.

        In particular, employers and economists may never be able to distinguish between sorting by unmeasured human capital and efficiency wages. In both cases, higher wages improve worker productivity. Whether the resulting productivity boost arises from attracting employees of better quality or from bringing out the best in otherwise normal workers promises to defy the data and methodology available to economists for the foreseeable future.

19.   See Aoki (1984) or Edwards (1979) for two models of nonunion bargaining.

20.   Studies of rent capture as an explanation for industry-wage differentials vary in whether they measure market power by four-firm concentration ratio (which may not be an accurate measure) or profit rate (which is reduced as wages rise, and varies with accounting practices), and in the other factors they include as control variables. Dickens and Katz (1987a) review this literature. Most studies find a positive relationship between industry wages and profit rates, controlling for human capital and union status, and sometimes establishment size and capital intensity. Even more studies also find a positive relationship between industry concentration and wages, controlling for union status and a variety of industry characteristics, although these findings are sometimes attenuated by the inclusion of human-capital controls. Another strand of literature finds evidence of union workers' ability to capture corporate rents. See Hirsch and Connally (1987) for a critical review of this literature.

21.   For example, see "Small Companies Lead the Way as Massachusetts Rebounds," *New York Times*, January 27, 1995.

22.   These categories, somewhat more aggregate than would be necessitated by the 1993 data, are needed to facilitate comparison between the 1993 and 1979 results.

23.   The two pension questions used for this study, quoting from the Census questionnaire, were:
        39. Now, I'd like to ask about retirement plans on your job – not government programs like Social Security, but employer-sponsored plans. This includes regular pensions. It also includes other plans where money is accumulated in an individual account for retirement – like thrift, savings, profit-sharing or stock plans. First, does your employer or union have any such pension or retirement plan for anyone in your (company/organization)?
        40. Are you included?

        The questions for health insurance were:
        61. Turning now to health insurance, does your employer offer a health insurance plan to any of its employees'?
        62. Are you covered by this health insurance plan?

24.   Dropping the industry dummies is required to capture the effects of industry rents and bargaining. If the industry dummies were retained, the union density coefficient would measure the effects of union density within broad industry groupings.

25.   The two notable changes in the surveys are the shift in the measure of education and establishment size. In the earlier survey education was reported as years of schooling completed; in 1993 the survey provided categorical information on educational attainment, particularly attainment of degrees. There were also changes in the coding of establishment size: the 1993 coding provided more detail on small establishments, but lumped all establishments with 250 or more employees into a single category. This has caused some discontinuities in measures of establishment size between 1979 and 1993.

26.   The category "white" would more accurately be called non-African American. The category includes Caucasians, Asians, non-black Hispanics, and all other non-African American employees.

BIBLIOGRAPHY

Abowd, John M. 1989. "The Effect of Wage Bargains on the Stock Market Value of the Firm." *American Economic Review*, 79 (September), pp. 774-809.

Akerlof, George A. 1981. "Jobs as Dam Sites." *Review of Economic Studies*, 48 (January), pp. 37-49.

Akerlof, George A. 1982. "Labor Contracts as Partial Gift Exchange." *Quarterly Journal of Economics*, 97 (November), pp. 543-69.

Akerlof, George A. 1984. "Gift Exchange and Efficiency Wage Theory: Four Views." *American Economic Review*, 74 (May), pp. 79-83.

Akerlof, George A., and Janet L. Yellen. 1986. *Efficiency Wage Models of the Labor Market*. Cambridge, U.K.: Cambridge University Press.

Antos, Joseph R. 1983. "Union Effects on White Collar Compensation." *Industrial and Labor Relations Review*, 36 (April), pp. 461-79.

Aoki, Masahiko. 1984. *The Cooperative Game Theory of the Firm*. New York: Oxford University Press.

Atrostic, B.K. 1983. "Alternative Pay Measures and Labor Market Differentials." Working Paper No. 127, U. S. Department of Labor, Office of Research and Evaluation, Bureau of Labor Statistics, Washington, D.C.

Azariadis, Costas. 1983. "Employment With Asymmetric Information." *Quarterly Journal of Economics*, 98 (Supplement), pp. 157-72.

Barron, John M., Dan A. Black, and Mark A. Loewenstein. 1987. "Employer Size: The Implications for Search, Training, Capital Investment, Starting Wages, and Wage Growth." *Journal of Labor Economics*, 5, pp. 76-89.

Barth, James R., Joseph J. Cordes, and Sheldon E. Haber. 1987. "Employee Characteristics and Firm Size: Are There Systematic Empirical Relationships?" *Applied Economics*, 19, pp. 555-67.

Becker, Gary. 1964. *Human Capital*. Cambridge, Mass.: National Bureau of Economic Research.

Belman, Dale, and John S. Heywood. 1990. "The Effect of Establishment and Firm Size on Public Wage Differentials." *Public Finance Quarterly*, 18 (April), pp. 221-35.

Blackburn, McKinley, and David Neumark. 1988. "Efficiency Wages, Inter-Industry Wage Differentials, and the Returns to Ability." *Finance and Economics Discussion Series,* No. 32, Federal Reserve Board, Washington, D.C.

Blanchflower, David G., and Andrew J. Oswald. 1990. "The Determination of White-Collar Pay." *Oxford Economic Papers*, 42, pp. 356-78.

Blanchflower, David G., Andrew J. Oswald, and Mario D. Garrett. 1990. "Insider Power in Wage Determination." *Economica,* 57 (May), pp. 143-70.

Blau, Francine. 1977. *Equal Pay in the Office*. Lexington, Mass: D.C. Heath and Co.

Brown, Charles. 1980. "Equalizing Differences in the Labor Market." *Quarterly Journal of Economics*, 94 (February), pp. 113-34.

Brown, Charles, James Hamilton, and James Medoff. 1990. *Employers Large and Small*. Cambridge, Mass.: Harvard University Press.

Brown, Charles, and James L. Medoff. 1989. "The Employer Size Wage Effect." *Journal of Political Economy*, 97 (October), pp. 1027-59.

Brown, William, John Hayles, Barry Hughes, and Lyndon Rowe. 1984. "Production and Labor Markets in Wage Determination: Some Australian Evidence." *British Journal of Industrial Relations*, 22 (July), pp. 169-76.

Buckley, John E. 1979. "Do Area Wages Reflect Area Living Costs?" *Monthly Labor Review*, 102 (November), pp. 24-9.

Bulow, Jeremy I., and Lawrence H. Summers. 1986. "A Theory of Dual Labor Markets With Application to Industrial Policy, Discrimination, and Keynesian Unemployment." *Journal of Labor Economics*, 4 (July), pp. 376-414.

Cain, Glenn G. 1976. "The Challenge of Segmented Labor Market Theories to Orthodox Theory." *Journal of Economic Literature*, 14 (December), pp. 1215-57.

Conant, Eaton H. 1963. "Worker Efficiency and Wage Differentials in a Clerical Labor Market." *Industrial and Labor Relations Review*, 16 (April), pp. 428-33.

Dalton, James A., and E. J. Ford Jr. 1977. "Concentration and Labor Earnings in Manufacturing and Utilities." *Industrial and Labor Relations Review*, 31 (October), pp. 45-60.

Davis, Steve J., and John Haltiwanger. 1991. "Wage Dispersion Between and Within U.S. Manufacturing Plants: 1963-86; Comments and Discussion." *Brookings Papers on Economic Activity*, Brookings Institution, Washington, D.C., pp. 115-200.

Dickens, William T. 1986. "Wages, Employment and the Threat of Collective Action by Workers." Working Paper No. 1856, National Bureau of Economic Research, Cambridge, Mass.

Dickens, William T., and Lawrence F. Katz. 1987a. "Industry Wage Differences and Theories of Wage Determination." Working Paper No. 2271, National Bureau of Economic Research, Cambridge, Mass.

Dickens, William T., and Lawrence F. Katz. 1987b. "Industry Wage Differences and Industry Characteristics." In Kevin Lang and Jonathon S. Leonard, eds, *Unemployment and the Structure of Labor Markets.* New York, N.Y.: Basil Blackwell Inc., pp. 48-89.

Dickens, William T., and Kevin Lang. 1985. "A Test of Dual Labor Market Theory." *American Economic Review*, 75 (September), pp. 792-805.

Dickens, William T., and Kevin Lang. 1985. "Testing Dual Labor Market Theory: A Reconsideration of the Evidence." Working Paper No. 1670, National Bureau of Economic Research, Cambridge, Mass.

Dickens, William T., and Kevin Lang. 1986. "Labor Market Segmentation and the Union Wage Premium." Working Paper No. 1883, National Bureau of Economic Research, Cambridge, Mass.

Doeringer, Peter B., and Michael J. Piore. 1971. *Internal Labor Markets and Manpower Analysis.* Lexington, Mass: D.C. Heath and Co.

Dunlop, John T. 1957. "The Task of Contemporary Wage Theory." In G. Taylor and F. Pierson, eds., *New Concepts in Wage Determination.* New York, N.Y.: McGraw-Hill.

Dunlop, John T. 1982. "Fundamentals of Wages and Labor Markets." Unpublished paper, Harvard University.

Dunn, Lucia. 1980. "The Effects of Firm and Plant Size on Employee Well-Being." In John Siegfried, ed., *The Economics of Firm Size, Market Structure and Social Performance.* Washington, D.C.: Federal Trade Commission.

Dunn, Lucia. 1980. "Work Disutility and Compensating Differentials: Estimation of Factors in the Link Between Wages and Firm Size." *Review of Economics and Statistics*, 68, pp. 67-73.

Dunn, Lucia. 1984. "The Effects of Firm Size on Wages, Fringe Benefits, and Worker Disutility." In Harvey Goldschmidt, et al., eds., *The Impact of the Modern Corporation.* New York, N.Y.: Columbia Press.

Dunne, Timothy, and James A. Schmitz. 1992. "Wages, Employment Structure and Employer Size Wage Premia: Their Relationship to Advanced Technology Usage at U.S. Manufacturing Companies." Discussion Paper No. 92015, Bureau of the Census, Center for Economic Studies, Washington, D.C.

Dunne, Timothy, and James A. Schmitz. 1994. "Wages, Employment Structure and Employer Size Wage Premia: Their Relationship to Advanced Technology Usage at U.S. Manufacturing Companies." *Economica* 62 (February), pp. 89-107.

Eberts, Randall W., and Joe A. Stone. 1985. "Wages, Fringe Benefits and Working Conditions: An Analysis of Compensating Differentials." *Southern Economic Journal*, 52 (July), pp. 274-80.

Edwards, Richard. 1979. *Contested Terrain.* New York, N.Y.: Basic Books.

Ehrenberg, Ronald G., and George T. Milkovich. 1987. "Compensation and Firm Performance." In Morris Kleiner, et al., eds., *Human Resources and the Performance of the Firm.* Madison, Wis.:, Industrial Relations Research Association, pp. 87-122.

Evans, David S. 1987. "The Relationship Between Firm Growth, Size, and Age: Estimates for 100 Manufacturing Industries." *Journal of Industrial Economics*, 35 (June), pp. 567-81.

Evans, David S., and Linda S. Leighton. 1989. "Why Do Smaller Firms Pay Less?" *Journal of Human Resources*, 24 (Spring), pp. 299-318.

Evans, Robert Jr. 1961. "Worker Quality and Wage Dispersion: An Analysis of a Clerical Labor Market in Boston." *Industrial Relations Research Association Proceedings*, New York, December 28-29, pp. 246-59.

Even, William E. 1992. "Determinants of Parental Leave Policies." *Applied Economics*, 24 (January), pp. 35-43.

Freeman, Richard B. 1981. "The Effect of Unionism on Fringe Benefits." *Industrial and Labor Relations Review*, 34 (July), pp. 489-509.

Garbarino, Joseph W. 1950. "A Theory of Interindustry Wage Structure Variation." *Quarterly Journal of Economics*, 64 (May), pp. 282-305.

Garen, John E. 1985. "Worker Heterogeneity, Job Security, and Firm Size." *Journal of Political Economy*, 93 (August) pp. 715-39.

Gibbons, Robert, and Lawrence Katz. 1987. "Learning, Mobility, and Interindustry Wage Differentials." Massachusetts Institute of Technology, Cambridge, Mass., unpublished paper.

Gibbons, Robert, and Lawrence Katz. 1989. "Does Unmeasured Ability Explain Interindustry Wage Differentials?" Working Paper No. 3182, National Bureau of Economic Research, Cambridge, Mass.

Griliches, Zvi. 1969. "Capital-Skill Complementarity."

Griliches, Zvi. 1970. "Notes on the Role of Education in Production Functions and Growth Accounting." In W. Lee Hansen, ed., *Education , Income, and Human Capital* New York, N.Y.: National Bureau of Economic Research.

Griliches, Zvi. 1979. "Sibling Models and Data in Economics: Beginnings of a Survey." *Journal of Political Economy*, 87, pp. S37-S64.

Groshen, Erica L. 1989. "Do Wage Differences Among Employers Last?" Working Paper No. 8906, Federal Reserve Bank of Cleveland.

Groshen, Erica L. 1990. "Ability to Pay, Rent Capture, and Salaries in the Private Sector." Proceedings of the Fortieth Annual Meeting, Industrial Relations Research Association, Madison, Wis., pp. 186-94.

Groshen, Erica L. 1991a. "Sources of Intra-Industry Wage Dispersion: How Much Do Employers Matter?" *Quarterly Journal of Economics* (August).

Groshen, Erica L. 1991b. "Five Reasons Why Wages Vary Among Employers." Industrial Relations Research Association (Fall).

Groshen, Erica L., and Alan B. Krueger. 1990. "The Structure of Supervision and Pay in Hospitals." *Industrial and Labor Relations Review*, 43 (February), pp. S143-46.

Hamermesh, Daniel S. 1980. "Commentary." In John Siegfried, ed., *The Economics of Firm Size, Market Structure and Social Performance*. Washington, D.C.: Federal Trade Commission.

Hamermesh, Daniel S. 1993. *Labor Demand*, Princeton, N.J.: Princeton University Press.

Helwege, Joan. 1989. "Sectoral Shifts and Interindustry Wage Differentials." Finance and Economics Discussion Series No. 102, Federal Reserve Board, Washington, D.C.

Hirsch, Barry T., and Robert A. Connally. 1987. "Do Unions Capture Monopoly Profits?" *Industrial and Labor Relations Review*, 41 (October), pp. 118-36.

Hodson, Randy. 1983. *Workers' Earnings and Corporate Economic Structure*. New York: Academic Press.

Holmstrom, Bengt. 1983. "Equilibrium Long-Term Labor Contracts." *Quarterly Journal of Economics*, 98 (Supplement), pp. 23-54.

Holtman, A.G., and Todd L. Idson. 1993. Wage Determination of Registered Nurses in Proprietary Nursing Homes." *Journal of Human Resources,* 28 (Winter), pp. 55-79.

Holzer, Harry. 1990. "Wages, Employer Costs, and Employee Performance in the Firm." *Industrial and Labor Relations Review*, 43 (February), pp. S147-64.

Idson, Todd L. 1990. "Establishment Size, Job Satisfaction and the Structure of Work." *Applied Economics*, 22 (August), pp. 1007-18.

Idson, Todd L. 1995. "Employer Size and Labor Turnover." *Research in Labor Economics*, 15.

Idson, Todd L., and Daniel J. Feaster. 1990. "A Selectivity Model of Employer Size Wage Differentials." *Journal of Labor Economics,* Vol. 8, January, pp. 99-122.

Jovanovic, Boyan. 1979. "Firm-Specific Human Capital." *Journal of Political Economy*, 87 (December), pp. 1246-60.

Jovanovic, Boyan. 1979. "Job Matching and the Theory of Turnover." *Journal of Political Economy*, 87 (October), pp. 972-90.

Katz, Lawrence. 1986. "Efficiency Wage Theories: A Partial Evaluation." In Stanley Fischer, ed., *NBER Macroeconomics Annual*. Cambridge, Mass.: MIT Press, pp. 235-75.

Kerr, Clark. 1983. "The Intellectual Role of Neorealists in Labor Economics." *Industrial Relations*, 22 (Spring), pp. 298-318.

Kleiner, Morris M., and Marvin L. Boullion. 1988. "Providing Business Information to Production Workers: Correlates of Compensation and Profitability." *Industrial and Labor Relations Review*, 41 (July), pp. 605-17.

Kostiuk, Peter F. 1990. "Firm Size and Executive Compensation." *Journal of Human Resources*, 25 (Winter), pp. 90-105.

Kremer, Michael, and Eric Maskin. 1994. "Segregation by Skill and the Rise in Inequality." unpublished paper, Harvard University.

Krueger, Alan B. 1987. "Ownership, Agency, and Wages: An Empirical Analysis." Unpublished paper, Princeton University.

Krueger, Alan B., and Lawrence H. Summers. 1987. "Reflections on the Inter-Industry Wage Structure." In Kevin Lang and Jonathan S. Leonard, eds., *Unemployment and the Structure of Labor Markets*, New York, N.Y.: Basil Blackwell Inc., pp. 17-47.

Krueger, Alan B., and Lawrence H. Summers. 1988. "Efficiency Wages and the Inter-Industry Wage Structure," *Econometrica*, 56 (March), pp. 259-93.

Kruse, Douglas. 1991. "Supervision, Working Conditions, and the Employer Size–wage Effect." *Journal of Industrial Relations*, 33 (September), pp. 229-49.

Lang, Kevin. 1987. "Persistent Wage Dispersion and Involuntary Unemployment." Unpublished paper, Boston University.

Lang, Kevin, and William T. Dickens. 1987. "Neoclassical and Sociological Perspectives on Segmented Labor Markets." Working Paper No. 2127, National Bureau of Economic Research, Cambridge, Mass.

Leonard, Jonathan S. 1987. "Carrots and Sticks: Pay, Supervision and Turnover," *Journal of Labor Economics*, 5 (October), pp. S136-52.

Leonard, Jonathan S. 1989. "Wage Structure and Dynamics in the Electronics Industry." *Industrial Relations*, 28 (Spring), pp. 251-75.

Lester, Richard A. 1952. "A Range Theory of Wage Differentials," *Industrial and Labor Relations Review*, 5 (July), pp. 483-500.

Lester, Richard A. 1967. "Pay Differentials by Size of Establishment," *Industrial Relations*, 7 (October), pp. 57-67.

Levine, David I. 1991. "Can Wage Increases Pay for Themselves? Tests with a Production Function," Unpublished paper, University of California, Berkeley.

Levine, David I. 1991. "You Get What You Pay For: Tests of Efficiency Wages Theories in the United States and Japan," Unpublished paper, University of California, Berkeley.

Lewis, L. Earl. 1956. "Wage Dispersion in Manufacturing Industries 1950-1955," *Monthly Labor Review*, 79 (July), pp. 780-6.

Lindbeck, Assar, and Dennis J. Snower. 1987. "Efficiency Wages Versus Insiders and Outsiders." *European Economic Review*, 31, pp. 407-16.

Mackay, Donald I., David Boddy, John Brack, John A. Diack, and Norman Jones. 1971. *Labour Markets Under Different Employment Conditions*. London: George Allen & Unwin Ltd.

Masters, Stanley H. 1969. "An Interindustry Analysis of Wages and Plant Size." *Review of Economics and Statistics*, 51 (August), pp. 341-5.

Mayo, John W., and Matthew N. Murray. 1991. "Firm Size, Employment Risk and Wages: Further Insights on a Persistant Puzzle." *Applied Economics*, 23 (August), pp. 1351-9.

Medoff, James L., and Katherine G. Abraham. 1980. "Experience, Performance and Earnings." *Quarterly Journal of Economics*, 95 (December), pp. 703-36.

Mellow, Wesley. 1982. "Employer Size and Wages." *Review of Economics and Statistics*, 64 (August), 495-504.

Miller, Edward M. 1981. "Variation of Wage Rates With Size of Establishment," *Economic Letters*, 8, pp. 281-6.

Miller, Edward M. 1987. "A Comparison of Large and Small Firm Productivity, Labor Compensation, and Investment Rates." *Review of Business and Economic Research*, 23, (Fall), pp. 26-37.

Mincer, Jacob. 1974. *Schooling, Experience, and Earnings.* New York: National Bureau Economic Research.

Montgomery, Edward, Kathryn Shaw, and Mary Ellen Benedict. 1992. "Pensions and Wages: An Hedonic Price Theory Approach." *International Economic Review*, 33 (February), 111-28.

Montgomery, James. 1987. "Equilibrium Wage Dispersion and Interindustry Wage Differentials." Unpublished paper, Massachusetts Institute of Technology.

Murphy, Kevin M., and Robert H. Topel. 1987. "Unemployment, Risk, and Earnings: Testing for Equalizing Wage Differences in the Labor Market." In Kevin K Lang and Jonathan S. Leonard, eds., *Unemployment and the Structure of Labor Markets*, New York, N.Y.: Basil Blackwell Inc., pp. 103-41.

Nolan, Peter, and William Brown. 1983. "Competition and Work Place Wage Determination." *Oxford Bulletin of Economics and Statistics*, 45 (August), pp. 269-87.

Oi, Walter Y. 1962. "Labor as a Quasi-Fixed Factor." *Journal of Political Economy*, 70, pp. 538-55.

Oi, Walter Y. 1983. "The Fixed Costs of Specialized Labor." In Jack Triplett, ed., *The Measurement of Labor Costs.* Chicago, Ill.: University of Chicago Press (for National Bureau of Economic Research).

Oi, Walter Y. 1990. "Employment Relations in Dual Labor Markets ("It's Nice Work If You Can Get It")." *Journal of Labor Economics*, 8 (January), pp. 124-49.

Pearce, James E. 1990. "Tenure, Unions, and the Relationship Between Employer Size and Wages." *Journal of Labor Economics*, 8 (April), pp. 251-69.

Pencavel, John. 1970. *An Analysis of the Quit Rate in the American Manufacturing Industry.* Princeton, N.J.: Industrial Relations Section, Princeton University.

Perlman, Jacob. 1940. "Hourly Earnings of Employees in Large and Small Enterprises." Monograph 14, Temporary National Economic Committee, U.S. Government Printing Office, Washington, D.C.

Personick, Martin E., and Carl B. Barsky. 1982. "White Collar Pay Levels Linked to Corporate Work Force Size." *Monthly Labor Review*, 105 (May), pp. 23-8.

Pugel, Thomas A. 1980. "Profitability, Concentration and the Interindustry Variation in Wages." *Review of Economics and Statistics*, 62 (May), pp. 248-53.

Raff, Daniel M.G., and Lawrence H. Summers. 1987. "Did Henry Ford Pay Efficiency Wages?" *Journal of Labor Economics*, 5 (October), pp. S57-86.

Rees, Albert, and George P. Schultz. 1970. *Workers and Wages in An Urban Labor Market.* Chicago, Ill.: University of Chicago Press.

Reynolds, Lloyd G. 1951. *The Structure of Labor Markets.* New York, N.Y.: Harper & Brothers.

Reynolds, Lloyd G., and Cynthia Taft. 1956. *The Evolution of Wage Structure.* New Haven, Conn.: Yale Press.

Rosen, Sherwin. 1969. "On the Interindustry Wage and Hours Structure." *Journal of Political Economy*, 77 (March-April), pp. 249-73.

Rothschild, Michael, and Joseph E. Stiglitz. 1976. "Equilibrium in Competitive Insurance Markets: An Essay on the Economics of Imperfect Information." *Quarterly Journal of Economics*, 90 (November), pp. 629-49.

Roy, Andrew D. 1951. "Some Thoughts on the Distribution of Earnings." *Oxford Economic Papers*, 3 (June), pp. 135-46.

Salop, Steven C. 1979. "A Model of the Natural Rate of Unemployment." *American Economic Review*, 69 (March), pp. 117-25.

Sattinger, Michael. 1980. *Capital and the Distribution of Labor Earnings.* New York, N.Y.: North Holland.

Schaffner, Julie Anderson. 1993. "Employer Size, Wages and the Nature of Employment in Peru." Unpublished paper, Stanford University.

Schmidt, Christopher M., and Klaus F. Zimmerman. 1991. "Work Characteristics, Firm Size and Wages." *Review of Economics and Statistics*, 73 (November), pp. 705-10.

Segal, Martin. 1986. "Post-Institutionalism in Labor Economics: The Forties and Fifties Revisited." *Industrial and Labor Relations Review*, 39 (April), pp. 388-403.

Seiler, Eric. 1982. "Piece Rate vs. Time Rate: The Effect of Incentives on Earnings." Working Paper No. 879, National Bureau of Economic Research, Cambridge, Mass.

Shapiro, Carl, and Joseph E. Stiglitz. 1984. "Equilibrium Unemployment as a Worker Discipline Device." *American Economic Review*, 74 (June), pp. 433-4.

Slichter, Sumner. 1950. "Notes on the Structure of Wages." *Review of Economics and Statistics*, 32 (February), pp. 80-91.

Smith, Adam. 1982. *The Wealth of Nations*. (1776). Penguin English Library Edition.

Smith, Robert S. 1979. "Compensating Wage Differentials and Public Policy: A Review." *Industrial and Labor Relations Review*, 32 (April), pp. 339-52.

Smith, Robert S., and Ronald G. Ehrenberg. 1981. "Estimating Wage-Fringe Trade-Offs: Some Data Problems." Working Paper No. 827, National Bureau of Economic Research, Cambridge, Mass.

Spence, A. Michael. 1973. "Job Market Signalling." *Quarterly Journal of Economics*, 87 (May), pp. 355-75.

Stigler, George J. 1962. "Information in the Labor Market." *Journal of Political Economy*, 70 (October), pp. S94-105.

Stiglitz, Joseph E. 1979. "On Search and Equilibrium Price Distributions." In Michael J. Posken, ed., *Economics of Human Welfare*. New York, N.Y.: Academic Press.

Stiglitz, Joseph E. 1984. "Theories of Wage Rigidities." Working Paper No. 1442, National Bureau of Economic Research, Cambridge, Mass.

Straka, John W. 1989. "Efficiency Wages and Collective Bargaining: Theory and Evidence" Ph.D. dissertation, Cornell University.

Strand, Jon. 1987. "The Relationship Between Wages and Firm Size: An Information Theoretic Analysis." *International Economic Review*, 28 (February), pp. 51-68.

Topel, Robert H. 1984. "Equilibrium Earnings, Turnover and Unemployment." *Journal of Labor Economics*, 2 (October), pp. 500-22.

Troske, Kenneth R. 1994. "Evidence on the Employer Size–wage Premium From Worker Establishment Data." Unpublished paper, Center for Economic Studies, U.S. Census Bureau, Washington, D.C.

Van Giezen, Robert W. 1982. "A New Look At Occupational Wages Within Individual Establishments." *Monthly Labor Review*, 105 (November), pp. 22-8.

Venables, Anthony J. 1983. "Random Job Prospects and the Distribution of Income." *Quarterly Journal of Economics*, 98 (November), pp. 637-57.

Wachtel, Howard M., and Charles Betsey. 1972. "Employment at Low Wages." *Review of Economics and Statistics*, 54 (May), pp. 121-9.

Wachter, Michael L. 1970. "Cyclical Variation in the Interindustry Wage Structure." *American Economic Review*, 60 (March), pp. 75-84.

Wadhwani, Sushil and Martin Wall. 1988. "A Direct Test of the Efficiency Wage Model Using UK Micro-Data." Working Paper No. 1022, London School of Economics Centre for Labour Economics.

Ward, Virginia L. 1980. "Measuring Wage Relationships Among Selected Occupations." *Monthly Labor Review*, 103 (May), pp. 21-5.

Weiss, Leonard A. 1966. "Concentration and Labor Earnings." *American Economic Review*, 56 (March), pp. 96-117.

Weitzman, Martin. 1986. *The Share Economy: Conquering Stagflation*. Cambridge, Mass.: Harvard University Press.

Yellen, Janet L. 1984. "Efficiency Wage Models of Unemployment." *American Economic Review*, 74 (May), pp. 200-5.

PART 2

Small Business Employment Dynamics Revisited

BY DAVID W. STEVENS AND JULIA LANE

The authors wish to thank Jared Bernstein and Larry Mishel of the Economic Policy Institute for comments on a draft manuscript. The authors accept full responsibility for the results, opinions, and conclusions that appear here.

INTRODUCTION

"Small Business Creates Ninety-Five Percent of New Jobs," reports a recent newsletter, citing new figures from the Small Business Administration.[1] This is the latest statement in a blizzard of new assertions that have appeared in the last several years about small business employment dynamics.[2] The goal of this study is to provide nonspecialists an introduction to the insights that have emerged from this research effort. Our own findings, from an analysis of a new database, complement these advances.

Interest in the role of small businesses in the U.S. economy has escalated since the sweeping Republican gains in the November 1994 elections. Issues such as regulatory reform, tort reform, amendment of capital gains tax laws, treatment of health care costs for the self-employed, the introduction of education vouchers for adult workers, and pending redefinitions of eligibility criteria and performance standards for federal welfare and employment and training programs promise to heighten partisan advocacy relating to the small business sector.

It will be important in these battles to separate fact from fiction. This paper focuses on what is likely to be one of the most contentious aspects of the debate: the historical and projected contribution of the small business sector to the nation's pool of stable and rewarding jobs.

Nearly 20 years ago, David Birch (1979) fueled an aggressive campaign of small business advocacy that was to gain steam during the Reagan Administration. The virtuousness of small business quickly became conventional wisdom. The pendulum has since swung in the other direction, however, producing a burst of critical attention in the last two or three years.

We treat these new contributions as a platform upon which to present our own findings. We begin with concepts and definitions, and then examine the fundamental characteristics of the databases that have been relied upon by different authors. We offer highlights of these authors' findings, and then turn to a presentation and interpretation of our own new evidence.

Along the way, we attempt to provide some context to the issue of small business employment dynamics. Often, an accurate understanding of one feature of this field requires an ability to place an isolated finding within a more complete mosaic of economic institutions and behavior. For example, some writers focus on the small business community's contribution to job *creation* without acknowledging simultaneous job *destruction*. Similarly, researchers often blur the distinction between *gross* and *net* job creation, while introducing job creation *rate* figures when it suits their purposes. Indeed, the definition of "small" tends to vary, even in different works by the same author.

The goal of this study is to provide nonspecialists an introduction to the insights that have emerged from the study of small business employment dynamics.

A single criterion guides our examination of concepts and findings reported by others and the development of our own findings and conclusions drawn from new evidence – *what might the ramifications be of relying on this concept, or finding, by itself, for decision-making purposes?* This criterion can be split into two component parts: a *transparency* criterion: "Is a nonspecialist likely to understand and use the standalone finding properly?" and an *actionability* criterion: "Is there an obvious use to which this new information can be put?"

Eberts and Montgomery (1994) and Davis and Haltiwanger (1994) use similar language to describe the underlying motivation for advancing the frontier of what can be said about job and worker flows. Workers are described as responding to forces that are associated with the relative attractiveness of different job/employer affiliations, while employers are seen as responding to forces linked to consumer demand, the extent of competition, and the relative costs and availability of labor and capital resources. The worker flows have been stylized in supply (matching) models, while job flows have been elaborated in demand/factor-cost models. Like those authors, we concentrate on demand-side dynamics, as these constrain and interact with the opportunity and incentive for workers to improve their circumstances by changing employer affiliation (or employment status). This is the motivation for what follows: What can be said about small business employment dynamics as they might affect employee opportunities to share in the nation's prosperity?

What can be said about small business employment dynamics as they might affect employee opportunities to share in the nation's prosperity?

CONCEPTS AND DEFINITIONS

There are four components of any change in *net* employment (Grey 1994, 64): (1) gains from business openings; (2) gains from business expansions; (3) losses from business contractions; and (4) losses from business closings. Virtually every word used in describing these components is subject to different interpretations, and these differences are imbedded in the datasets that have been used to examine small business employment dynamics. This is one reason why there has been little convergence of views among authors to date.

Eberts and Montgomery (1994, 15) describe two subtle measurement issues that make it difficult to compare findings reported in the literature. First, the *frequency of observation* affects the relative contribution of openings (or closings) and expansions (or contractions) to net employment gains (or losses).

> Given a time-invariant stochastic process of openings and closings, a greater proportion of employment gains would be attributed to openings than to expansions as the period between observations lengthens.

This phenomenon occurs because a longer interval between base-period and end-period observations permits more openings to occur while allowing more closings to remove what otherwise might have appeared as temporary expansions over a shorter interval. Thus, the allocation of observed net employment changes among the four components can be manipulated by choosing a particular reference interval.

The second measurement issue mentioned by Eberts and Montgomery (and others, including Davis and Haltiwanger 1994) is the applicable definition of an opening or closing. As Eberts and Montgomery note (1994, 15):

> From an economic perspective, one would define a "new establishment" as a newly created institution, typically located in one place, that combines labor, capital, and purchased inputs to produce goods or services. All studies basically agree with this definition. However, because of variations across datasets in the ability to track and identify firms, studies differ in implementing this definition, which is sensitive to the treatment of mergers and acquisitions, changes in management or ownership, and the movement of establishments from one location to another.

A sense of the importance of this measurement issue becomes apparent in two recent papers written by leading observers of small business employment dynamics. Davis, Haltiwanger, and Schuh (1994, 14) adopted the following unit of analysis:

> The basic observational unit underlying our job creation and destruction measures is the plant – a physical location where production takes place. In contrast to a plant, a company or firm is an economic and legal entity that encompasses one or more plants and, possibly, administrative offices specializing in nonproduction activities.

Virtually every word used in describing the components of change in net employment is subject to different interpretations.

63

Duncan and Handler (1994, 7, 9) are less willing to embrace this level of definitional precision:

> There is no official register or definition of new businesses. Unfortunately, a huge gray area exists between firms undertaking activities normally associated with a business and individuals merely acting to sell their own labor....
>
> When all of these casual or paper businesses are considered, the picture may be quite different because the startup was not real, the effort was not sustained or the idea was never workable. Thus many of these "casual" businesses undoubtedly fail in the first three years of life, giving rise to the myth of high rates of failure that is misunderstood as being representative of "real" small businesses.

Duncan and Handler distinguish between the *discontinuance* of a business (operations have ceased with no outstanding debts) and the *failure* of a business (operations have ceased with losses to creditors) as a refinement of the business *closing* concept. They also speak of *serious* businesses as a category distinct from other ventures.

What is the importance of these definitional nuances in terms of actionability? For instance, does it matter that Davis, Haltiwanger, and Schuh exclude from their definition administrative offices specializing in nonproduction activities? Does Duncan and Handler's exclusion of "...self-employed individuals or groups moving from venture to venture, which generally are not tracked by D&B" affect their findings and conclusions? These questions cannot be answered unless we know the particular use to which the reported findings are to be put. Moreover, no one should be lulled into a false sense of security by such reassuring assertions as this one by Dennis, Phillips, and Starr (1994, 25): "Counting jobs created (lost) by businesses of various sizes is a critical issue. Because no theoretical construct exists for counting, common-sensical decision rules were adopted from the outset by Birch, SBA, etc." A reader may agree with these "common-sensical" definitions but should probably wonder why there is no consensus about what constitutes "common-sensical" definitions.

Identification of the time interval between base-period and end-period observations and explicit definitions of the business unit of analysis and what constitutes an opening or closing are necessary but not sufficient components for understanding small business employment dynamics. Other pertinent components include the definition of *small*, the distinction between *gross* and *net* changes, and the difference between the turnover of *jobs* and the mobility of *workers*.

The Small Business Administration defines *small* as a business unit of analysis that has a recorded employment level of less than 500 at the time of observation. This explains the "small business creates 95 percent of new jobs" press re-

Identification of the time interval between base-period and end-period observations and explicit definitions of the business unit of analysis and what constitutes an opening or closing are necessary but not sufficient components for understanding small business employment dynamics.

lease, but only when the relevance of *boundary-crossing* units and the definition of *new jobs* are understood.

New jobs are identified by comparing the recorded number of incumbent employees in a business unit in base-period and end-period observations. *Boundary crossing* occurs when a business is classified in one employment-size class in the base-period observation and in a different class in the end period. Davis, Haltiwanger, and Schuh refer to a *size distribution fallacy* that arises from such boundary crossing. They assert that this is an important phenomenon that distorts estimates of small business job creation as businesses migrate from larger to smaller employment-size classes in particular economic circumstances. The actual importance and ramifications of this phenomenon are linked to a prior choice among base-period, end-period, or other (e.g., average) counts to assign a business entity to an employment-size class. We return to this topic when discussing data sources in the next section. The importance of the size-distribution fallacy depends on the empirical relevance of a related concept first described by Leonard (1987) – a *regression fallacy* or regression-to-the-mean bias. Davis, Haltiwanger, and Schuh trace this apparent bias to two sources: (1) transitory employment fluctuations and (2) measurement error. However, what the authors refer to as measurement error is contested by small business advocates, such as Dennis, Phillips, and Starr (1994, 26):

> The [SBA] counting process begins by tying all establishments (business locations) to their proper enterprises (business)....All enterprises are classified by employment size as of the base year....The process restarts at the end of every measuring period. Each enterprise is assigned a new size class (rebenched) based on the number of people it employs in the new base year (the old measuring year).

Davis, Haltiwanger, and Schuh (1994, 16-17) counter that:

> the interaction between this reclassification and transitory firm-level employment movements lies at the heart of the regression fallacy. On average, firms classified as large in the base year are more likely to have experienced a recent transitory increase in employment. Because transitory movements reverse themselves, firms that are large in the base year are relatively likely to contract. Likewise, firms classified as small in the base year are more likely to experience a recent transitory decrease in employment. Hence, firms that are small in the base year are relatively likely to expand. This regression phenomenon (i.e., regression to the firm's own long-run size) creates the illusion that small firms systematically outperform large firms.

The SBA employment-size-class ceiling of 499 is much higher than that used by many other authors. Davis, Haltiwanger, and Schuh use an employment-size class of 5-19 for most of their longitudinal analysis of employment dynamics in U.S. manufacturing plants. The SBA itself has focused on the employment-size

The SBA employment-size-class ceiling of 499 is much higher than that used by many other authors.

65

class 0-4 in some investigations of job creation and destruction in what is called the *micro*-business sector. Some comparative studies of international job creation patterns use an employment-size-class ceiling of 100. The important point for our purposes is that it is difficult to avoid apples-and-oranges comparisons.

The essence of the *gross* versus *net* employment change distinction is captured by Grey (1994, 1).

> The traditional focus on net employment growth hides much of the dynamics of employment creation: regardless of whether net employment is increasing or declining, large numbers of jobs are being created as well as destroyed. For the OECD [Organization for Economic Cooperation and Development] nations for which data are available, total [annual] turnover averaged more than 20% during the 1980s, although net employment growth was generally in the range 0.5-2%. In other words, each year an average of one in five jobs changed. Zero net employment growth can mask significant job gains and losses. Industries with declining employment can have significant job creation while industries with growing employment can have significant job losses.

Davis and Haltiwanger (1994, 5-9) provide a succinct catalog of pertinent concepts, including the following: "Gross *Job* Reallocation at time *t* equals the sum of all establishment-level employment gains and losses that occur between *t-1* and *t*. It equals the sum of job creation and destruction." They distinguish this concept of *job* reallocation from a related, but different, concept of worker flows: "Gross *Worker* Reallocation at time *t* equals the number of persons whose place of employment or employment status differs between *t-1* and *t*." This is a crucial distinction because most studies to date, and the datasets they have relied upon, count only jobs, or employment positions occupied by an incumbent, at the time of observation. A few studies and datasets, including the one introduced later in this paper, also permit workers to be identified and traced as they move from one employer to another. Davis and Haltiwanger (1994, 5) illustrate the importance of the issue. If two workers switch jobs (employers), then there have been two accessions and two separations (i.e., four transitions that are counted in total turnover). But the gross worker reallocation count is two – the number of workers whose place of employment has changed. Furthermore, if two incumbent workers exchange jobs within a single business entity, no transition is captured in either the gross worker reallocation or gross job reallocation concepts.

U.S. datasets, and researchers who use them, often focus on *ownership* in defining the business unit of analysis, while Eurostat's definition reflects an enterprise's *control* of a business unit (Grey 1994, 37). Harrison (1994, 47), however, refers to a recorded change of ownership through merger or acquisition as a "spurious" source of startup activity. This characterization surfaces in Harrison's development of a thesis expressed in the following:

If two workers switch jobs, then there have been four transitions that are counted in total turnover. But the gross worker reallocation count is two – the number of workers whose place of employment has changed.

In many cases the legally independent small firms from which the big companies purchase parts, components, and services may not be all that independent, after all, but should rather be treated as *de facto* branch plants belonging to the big firms. Production may be decentralized into a wider and more geographically far-flung number of work sites, but power, finance, and control remain concentrated in the hands of the managers of the largest companies in the global economy.

Again, the problem of concepts and definitions must be recognized. Up to this point, we have referred to *plants*, *establishments*, *enterprises*, *companies*, *casual* and *serious businesses*, and now *de facto branch plants*. Each might be judged to be the best choice for some types of inquiry, but an inappropriate selection for investigating other issues.[3]

FUNDAMENTALS OF U.S. DATA SOURCES

Some basics about the datasets used to date may be useful for our subsequent discussion of findings.

- The core data source used by Davis, Haltiwanger, and Schuh is the Longitudinal Research Datafile (LRD) maintained by the Census Bureau's Center for Economic Studies. This combines *plant-level* data from the Census of Manufactures, which has been conducted every five years, and the Annual Survey of Manufactures from non-Census years. The unit of analysis is manufacturing establishments. Plants with recorded employment levels of less than five are not included. The Census Bureau's Company Organization Survey data (for multi-unit enterprises) and the Social Security Administration's Employer Identification Numbers (for single-unit companies) have been used to trace the lifecycle of establishments whose longevity would be hidden by ownership changes reflected in some other data sources. The authors warn that "our ability to distinguish among startups, shutdowns and panel rotators [establishments that leave the probability sample every five years] is good, but not perfect. In addition, the exact timing of plant startups and shutdowns is difficult to pinpoint from LRD information. These problems complicate the task of measuring job creation and destruction..." (1994, 8).

- The Small Business Administration in the U.S. Department of Commerce has created two files from the Dun & Bradstreet Corporation's Dun's Marketing Identifier (DMI) file – the U.S. Establishment and Employment Microdata (USEEM) file, and the U.S. Establishment and Longitudinal Microdata (USELM) file. All establishments that have a D&B credit rating are included. A two-year time interval is used to reclassify enterprises by employment-size class. The longitudinal file is a stratified sample drawn from the USEEM file. Grey (1994, 36) and Davis and Haltiwanger (1994, 13-4) urge caution in the use of job creation and job destruction figures that are based on USELM data.[4]

- White and Osterman (1991) refined Wisconsin ES-202 quarterly filings by Milwaukee metro area employers between 1977 and 1987 to identify an establishment unit of analysis. This database was then used to estimate net change in employment figures for six employment-size classes. They first estimate within-size-class net change, and then look at the effect of cross-boundary growth or decline (i.e., an establishment that is assigned to one employment-size class in the base-period observation but to a different one in the end-period observation). This is an important contribution because it describes, as does a previous article by White et al. (1990), the detailed steps that must be followed to adjust raw quarterly employer reports to account for multi-establishment reporting biases. It also addresses something other than an actual production site (e.g., a payroll-processing firm, legal counsel's address, or accountant's location).

- The findings that we report later in this paper use Maryland ES-202 records similar to those used by White et al., but they are supplemented by the individual employee earnings records that are submitted to the state employment security agency in the second part of the dual purpose filing of quarterly contribution and wage reports. These data permit us to track both *job* and *worker* flows, recognizing the fuzziness of the desired distinction between an establishment (i.e., single production site) and an enterprise.[5]

Readers must stay alert to an author's use of alternative observation intervals. Davis, Haltiwanger, and Schuh (1994, 14) describe their approach:

> Our analysis considers four concepts: current plant size, average plant size, firm size and ownership type. Current size equals the simple average of the plant's current employment and its employment twelve months earlier. In contrast, average plant size equals the weighted mean number of employees, computed over all annual observations on the plant during the 1972 to 1988 period. Firm size equals the number of manufacturing workers employed by the parent firm in the preceding Census of Manufactures. Finally, ownership type indicates whether the plant's parent firm operates one or multiple plants.

The authors (1994, 14) assert that "...average plant size provides a better indication of the production unit's intended scale of operations. Hence, for most purposes, we prefer average size to current size." This is a controversial choice, as we show in a review of findings in the next section.

Thus, the reader of any of this literature should keep an eye out for a variety of different factors. The first are definitional: what is the frequency of measurement; what criteria are used to define a plant opening or closing; what measure is used to define size of firm; what cutoff is used to define "small"; and what definition of employment change is used – gross or net? The second set is the source of the data: how are the data selected; what period do they represent; and what sectors of the economy are covered? These are technical differences that can have a major impact on any policy conclusions.

The reader of this literature should keep an eye out for a variety of different factors. The first are definitional. The second set is the source of the data.

SMALL BUSINESS EMPLOYMENT DYNAMICS: RECENT FINDINGS[6]

Eberts and Montgomery (1994) report widespread agreement on three characteristics of small business employment dynamics:

- *Gross* employment flows are typically larger than *net* employment changes. The 20% annual *gross* flow rate reported by Grey (1994, 1) is commonly cited in the recent literature.

- Smaller businesses typically grow *faster* than their larger counterparts, but the meaning of this finding and its relevance for policy are open to debate.

- Substantial heterogeneity of employment growth/decline exists among establishments within an industry and among regions.

> *Smaller businesses typically grow faster than their larger counterparts, but the meaning of this finding and its relevance for policy are open to debate.*

Beyond these agreed-upon features of small business employment dynamics lies a much longer list of controversies. High on the list is the relative importance of business *openings* (*closings*) and *expansions* (*contractions*) to job creation (destruction). Eberts and Montgomery (1994) conclude that "employment gains from openings as a share of total job creation ranges from slightly more than 18% to nearly 71%." They cite two studies, Dunne et al. (1989) and Davis and Haltiwanger (1990), which used essentially the same Census Bureau database to arrive at figures of 60% and 20%, respectively, for job creation from *openings*. Eberts and Montgomery point out that "the primary reason for the disparity is that Dunne et al. attribute all employment growth during the five-year interval to new firms, while Davis and Haltiwanger attribute only the first year's growth to openings, with the rest attributed to expansions."

Berney and Phillips (1994) cite evidence from a forthcoming study of the Canadian manufacturing sector[7] that *net* employment change within the employment-size class 6-19 "...increased from 11.3% using the base-period size class assignment method over a one-year observation period to 53.9% using a five-year interval." Eberts and Montgomery (1994) cite a similar magnitude of difference between Leonard's finding that 18% of new jobs could be traced to openings (using ES-202 data for establishments with a one-year observation interval) versus Jacobson's attribution of 71% of new jobs to openings (using a similar database with a six-year observation interval.)

Berney and Phillips (1994) also cite Canadian findings reported in a second unpublished paper[8] that compares Davis, Haltiwanger, and Schuh's use of *average* employment (plant size as an indication of the production unit's intended scale of operations) to a new calculation of "average" that uses the employment level in a prior period as a substitute for the base-period observation and the employment level in the base period instead of the end period. The Canadian authors are reported to have concluded that this substitution of a prior/base average for Davis, Haltiwanger, and Schuh's base/end calculation produces "quite different magnitudes of change...so selecting the methodology more than just corrects the statistical problem; it affects the outcome." It is not clear, however, even if there were a statistical problem, that the substitution of a prior period's data for a current period's data is appropriate.

There is, however, no controversy about one effect of adopting the Davis, Haltiwanger, and Schuh concept of *average:* when compared with what Berney and Phillips refer to as the "traditional" base-period criterion for assigning a business unit to an employment-size class, their approach decreases the measured *gross* job gain and increases the measured *gross* job loss of small firms, so the resulting *net* job gain or loss will be smaller. Again, this occurs because transitory fluctuations move employment away from a longer-term "intended" level; the averaging calculation moves business units that have temporarily grown into a higher employment-size class and moves business units that have temporarily contracted into a lower one.

The importance of both the rule that is used to assign a business unit to an employment-size class and the boundary-crossing phenomenon is indicated by the magnitudes-of-change evidence contained in Berney and Phillips (1994, 16 and 19). It serves to indicate how the rules adopted by different authors can affect their results.

> Most of the 1.8 million firms which began life in this [0-4] size class remain in the same size class, creating only 310,000 jobs....Most of the job generation occurred in firms that started in the 0-4 class and ended in the 5-19 class (1.48 million jobs created).
>
> The boundary crossers, from SBA's point of view – that is, the firms that moved out of the small business category <500 into the large business category 500+ – only created 66 thousand jobs or 1.7% of jobs which were generated.

A particularly important topic from an actionability, policy-making standpoint is the separation of cyclical and secular components of job growth. Davis and Haltiwanger (1994), Dennis, Phillips, and Starr (1994), Eberts and Montgomery (1994), Gottschalk and Moffitt (1994), Grey (1994), and White and Osterman (1991) address this issue. There is some disagreement on the cyclicality of job growth. In particular, Davis and Haltiwanger find that (in manufacturing) job destruction is highly cyclical and job creation less so. Grey, on the other hand, argues that the datasets do not span a long enough period to identify cyclical effects. Other re-

A particularly important topic from a policy-making standpoint is the separation of cyclical and secular components of job growth.

71

searchers find different dynamics by region (Eberts and Montgomery) and by size class (Dennis, Phillips, and Starr). The jury is still out (according to Gottschalk and Moffitt) as to whether there has been a change in any employment dynamics over time. Highlights from recent studies demonstrate the extent to which the findings can vary:

The jury is still out as to whether there has been a change in any employment dynamics over time.

Davis and Haltiwanger (1994, 21-6)

- "Over the 1970s and 1980s job creation and job destruction are inversely correlated, job destruction varies much more over the cycle than does job creation, and job reallocation is countercyclical."

- "Job reallocation is countercyclical: the economy restructures the organization of employment positions in recessions. In contrast, turnover due to other factors is procyclical: the intensity with which workers sort across a given set of employment positions increases in booms. These two important but distinct components of total turnover thus have strikingly different cyclical properties."

- "Since only one-third of job destruction is accounted for by establishments that shrink by less than 25% over the span of a year, the bulk of job destruction cannot be accommodated by normal rates of worker attrition resulting from retirements and quits. In other words, most of the job destruction represents job loss from the point of view of workers."

Dennis, Phillips, and Starr (1994, 23-5)

- "The share of net jobs created by small (and large) businesses changes from measuring period to measuring period. This variation appears closely tied to the business cycle. Larger firms expand their share of net new employment toward the end of expansions. Small businesses provide a relatively stable supply throughout. Thus, variation in shares is primarily due to variations in large firm employment practices."

- "Jobs created from small business births are about two to three times as plentiful as the number created from small business expansions. This proportion seems to vary with the business cycle. Similarly, jobs lost in small businesses are primarily a function of business deaths rather than of business contractions."

- "The distribution of employment by firm size is changing rapidly across industries [small business importance growing in manufacturing and declining in retail trade]."

Eberts and Montgomery (1994)

- "Over the business cycle (short run), job destruction behavior seems to dominate, while across regions (long run), job creation may be relatively more important."

- "Consistent with previous studies, we find that net employment changes substantially understate the amount of turnover in the labor market. In 1976-78 and 1984-86, gross flows were five to eight times larger than net turnover, while in the recessionary period of 1980-82, they were more than 20 times bigger."

- "Within both growing and declining regions, significant amounts of creation and destruction are going on simultaneously. In expanding SMSAs [standard metropolitan statistical areas], almost 20% of jobs were lost in each of our data periods, while in contracting regions, enough new jobs were created in each period to increase employment by at least 15%....The same heterogeneity is displayed within industries."

Gottschalk and Moffitt (1994, 252-3)

- "For our purposes, the major question is whether these firm- and establishment-level dynamics have changed over time. On this point, the evidence is relatively weak. Davis and Haltiwanger, for example, find no trend from 1973 to 1986 in the sum of job creation and destruction rates in manufacturing. In addition, Dunne, Roberts, and Samuelson find no strong trend in plant-level turnover in manufacturing from 1963 to 1982."

- "While these studies reveal little evidence of trends in firm- and establishment-level employment turnover, the link between their findings and those we have presented [on earnings instability] is weakened by their exclusive focus on employment dynamics rather than wage dynamics. As we demonstrated previously, much of the increase in earnings volatility in the 1980s has arisen within jobs, and earnings instability has also increased for job stayers. This implies that earnings volatility should have increased even in the absence of changes in employment turnover and other employment fluctuations."

Grey (1994, 5-7)

- "While extensive work has been done to examine the impact that aggregate or transitory shocks have on turnover, the evidence is still mixed, and generalisations must be treated with some caution. In general, one would not expect job turnover to fluctuate over the economic cycle: job gains should be as likely to fall in recessions as job losses are to rise."

- "The difficulty in resolving the issue of the counter-cyclicality of turnover stems partly from the lack of sufficiently long time series to take account of the magnitude of movement over the cycle. The most significant movements in turnover, when structural change may have occurred, took place at only two points – the recessions of 1981-82 and 1990 or later. However, differences in turnover during these two periods from the remainder of the time series cannot be isolated."

- "Two perspectives have developed to explain why there might be a counter-cyclical pattern in job turnover. One emphasizes aggregate shocks as causes of recessions which alter the timing of job reallocation [recessions may be a time of 'cleaning up']. An alternative view suggests that major allocative shocks may be at the root of recessions and may be accompanied by sharp rises in job losses."

White and Osterman (1991, 256)

- "The importance of the role of the smallest or, for that matter, any size establishment varies with the period of analysis, including the segment of the business cycle, the industrial sector or specific industry or industry group examined, and the geographic location specified."

The lesson from these contrasting points of view is, perhaps, 'buyer beware.'

The lesson from these contrasting points of view is, perhaps, "buyer beware."

The next section presents our own new evidence using a data source that includes information about both businesses and their individual employees.

74

SMALL BUSINESS EMPLOYMENT DYNAMICS: 1987-93

The previous sections have discussed the difficulty in comparing studies conducted to date. Three sources of this difficulty are: (1) data source relied upon; (2) time interval(s) covered; and (3) definitions adopted. This study introduces yet another data source and covers a new, more recent, time interval.

The new information presented here covers an eight-year period, from 1985 to 1993, with attention concentrated on three quarterly snapshots – the third quarters of 1987, 1990, and 1993. The entire Maryland economy is represented, with the exception of federal government civilian and military units and personnel, self-employed individuals, and workers in particular niche sectors (e.g., railroads, religious and philanthropic organizations, and people who receive commissions only without a salary base).

Both single- and multi-establishment entities are included. The precise unit of analysis is the *employing unit* as defined for businesses that are required to file a quarterly contribution and wage report in compliance with the Unemployment Insurance Law of Maryland. More than 90% of the legal business entities in Maryland that are required to submit quarterly reports are single-establishment enterprises. For these, assignment to an employment-size class is unambiguous and consistent with the preferred definition described earlier.

The remaining relatively small number of multi-establishment businesses, which are concentrated in the retail trade and selected services sectors, cannot be described in so precise a manner. This introduces some fuzziness in the larger employment-size classes in the analysis that follows. Single large establishments and clusters of smaller establishments within a multi-establishment *employing unit* are combined, meaning that these establishments are omitted from the employment-size class to which they would have been assigned if their independent identity were known.[9] The *ownership* and *control* issue is pertinent in deciding how important this blurred boundary is from an actionability or policy-making standpoint. For many management decision-making and policy purposes it may make more sense to place individual establishments of a multi-establishment enterprise in the employment-size class that is consistent with the primary locus of management control. Harrison's concept of "independent" production units that are actually dependent on the behavior of a single large enterprise as being *de facto establishments* controlled by this larger enterprise simply extends this view one additional step.

The appendix describes steps we took to remove extremely short spells of worker affiliation with a particular employing unit. We cannot guarantee that all

> *The new information presented here covers an eight-year period, from 1985 to 1993, for the entire Maryland economy.*

TABLE 2-1
Distribution of firm characteristics by size category

	0-4	5-49	50-99	100-249	250-999	1000+
1987:3						
Number of firms	55.80%	38.36%	2.96%	1.82%	0.86%	0.20%
Total wages	5.47	24.08	9.56	12.49	17.82	30.58
Employment	6.28	25.68	9.51	12.83	18.07	27.62
1990:3						
Number of firms	57.74%	36.79%	2.84%	1.69%	0.76%	0.20%
Total wages	5.81	23.85	9.21	12.14	15.88	33.10
Employment	6.68	25.48	9.40	12.37	16.59	29.48
1993:3						
Number of firms	58.21%	36.19%	2.78%	1.83%	0.77%	0.21%
Total wages	5.76	23.25	9.00	12.77	16.12	33.09
Employment	6.40	24.47	9.10	13.07	16.72	30.25

Source: Authors' analysis of Maryland quarterly employment data.

employment spells of less than three months have been identified and removed, but we are comfortable in saying that the basic threshold time interval is a full quarter. Reasons for selecting the third quarter are also discussed in the appendix. Basically, first- and fourth-quarter data reflect well-known seasonal patterns of both employment and earnings. The timing of snapshots (1987, 1990, and 1993) offers different points in cyclical events and provides recent coverage.

Employment and earnings distributions by employment-size class

The topographical view of Maryland employment and earnings by employment-size class reveals no surprises. **Table 2-1** shows that more than 90% of Maryland businesses reported an average quarterly employment level of fewer than 50 workers in the third quarter of 1987, 1990, and 1993. This total probably understates the concentration of *establishments* in the smaller employment-size classes, since the multi-establishment reporting practice assigns component establishments to the larger employment-size classes.

The concentration of employing units in the smaller employment-size classes is not accompanied by corresponding distributions of total payroll figures or employment counts. The 0.2% of employing units that reported average employment levels of 1,000+ accounted for at least 31% of total payroll figures and 28% of total employment. The shares of total payroll and employment accounted for by the largest-size class grew slightly over the period 1987-93 – from 31% to 33% of total payroll and from 28% to 30% of total employment. The smallest employment-size class (0-4 paid employees), which contains more than 55% of Maryland's reporting employing units, accounts for only about 6% of total payrolls and employment. These employment-size distributions do not appear to have been affected by the combined forces of structural and cyclical events that occurred over the six-year period.

Gross job creation, destruction, reallocation, and net change

One important measure of job quality is stability – whether jobs last, measured by the reported number of incumbent workers.[10] The literature described earlier generally agrees that small businesses, however they have been defined, account for high levels of both job creation and job destruction. We proceed here to compare Maryland's flows of job creation and job destruction to a well-known example from the recent literature.

Four concepts from the earlier parts of this paper are used here. Each is expressed as a *rate*; that is, as a plus or minus change from a designated reference level. Following Davis and Haltiwanger (1992), we define a *gross job creation rate* as the ratio of the combined increases in reported employment counts at new and expanding employing units between a base period and an end period to the average of these base-period and end-period employment levels reported by these employing units. Similarly, we define a *gross job destruction rate* as the ratio of the combined decreases in employment at contracting employing units and those that stopped reporting during the reference period (deaths) to the average of the base-period and end-period employment levels reported. The *job reallocation rate* is the sum of these job creation and job destruction calculations. Finally, the *net job creation rate* is the ratio of the net change in the number of reported workers over the reference period to the average of the base-period and end-period observations.

The four ratios defined in the previous paragraph offer readers a relatively painless introduction to the distinct, but not independent, forces of job creation, job destruction, job "churning," or reallocation among employing units, and net contribution (+ or -) to employment growth. Our definition of the *net job creation rate* reflects a conscious acceptance of Davis and Haltiwanger's thesis that use of an average figure in the denominator of these ratio calculations is appropriate, because it limits the influence of transitory movements away from a desired, or normal, long-run employment level. This action is an explicit rejection of the superiority of a base-period, or prior/base-period average, calculation preferred by SBA advocates.

We begin with Davis, Haltiwanger, and Schuh's results for the U.S. manu-

One important measure of job quality is stability – whether jobs last, measured by the reported number of incumbent workers.

TABLE 2-2
Job creation, destruction, and reallocation in manufacturing, 1973-88

Current plant size	0-19	20-49	50-99	100-249	250-499	500-999	1000+
Share of total employment	5.2%	8.6%	10.5%	18.5%	16.0%	13.5%	27.7%
Net job creation	-4.5	-2.1	-1.3	-1.1	-1.0	-0.6	-0.8
Job creation rate	18.7	13.2	12.2	9.6	7.7	7.0	6.0
Job destruction rate	23.3	15.3	13.5	10.7	8.7	7.6	6.8
Gross job reallocation	42.0	28.5	25.7	20.3	16.4	14.6	12.8

Source: Davis, Haltiwanger, and Schuh (1993).

facturing sector using the Census Bureau's Longitudinal Research Datafile. **Table 2-2** reproduces highlights from their findings. The gross job creation rate over the 1973-88 reference period, by employment-size class, varied from a high of 18.7% for the smallest plants to a low of 6.0% for the largest plants of 1,000+ workers. This is one of the explanations for the often-repeated statement that "small business creates most of the new jobs in the United States." However, this pattern is complemented by a less-often-reported statistic – the gross job destruction rate of 23.3% is also highest for the smallest-size class and more than three times higher than the 6.8% gross job destruction rate for the largest-size class of 1,000+ workers. The sum of these gross job creation and gross job destruction rates is the *job reallocation rate*. Table 2-2 reveals that far more churning of job opportunities occurred in the smaller size classes in the U.S. manufacturing sector in the 1970s and early 1980s than occurred in the larger size classes – 42.0% in the smallest size class versus 12.8% in the largest size class. This churning is not revealed in the relatively small and similar negative rates of net job creation across the size classes, which range between -0.6% and -4.5% over this era of pervasive manufacturing decline in the United States.

Using quarterly Maryland wage record data, we update and extend Davis, Haltiwanger, and Schuh's findings for the manufacturing sector. These results are presented in **Tables 2-3** and **2-4**. The cyclical aspects of recent job flows are highlighted in these two tables, which compare Maryland's 1987:3, 1990:3, and 1993:3 job creation and job destruction rates. The manufacturing (Table 2-3) and nonmanufacturing (Table 2-4) sectors are separated so that we can compare our manufacturing sector findings directly with those of Davis, Haltiwanger, and Schuh (Table 2-2).[11]

Maryland's manufacturing sector dynamics in 1987-93 (Table 2-3) mirror the nation's recent manufacturing history (Table 2-2) in many respects.

78

TABLE 2-3
Manufacturing

	0-19	20-49	50-99	100-249	250-499	500-999	1000+
1987:3							
Net job creation rate	-1.16%	0.41%	1.79%	0.44%	2.85%	-14.46%	-2.03%
Job creation rate	13.46	10.10	10.82	6.31	7.91	1.35	0.17
Job destruction rate	14.62	9.69	9.03	5.87	5.06	15.81	2.19
Gross job reallocation rate	28.09	19.78	19.85	12.18	12.96	17.15	2.36
1990:3							
Net job creation rate	-2.09%	-4.28%	-9.43%	-3.69%	-2.90%	-13.51%	-3.03%
Job creation rate	12.50	10.47	5.35	3.75	2.05	1.23	0.39
Job destruction rate	14.59	14.75	14.78	7.44	4.95	14.73	3.41
Gross job reallocation rate	27.09	25.23	20.12	11.19	7.00	15.96	3.80
1993:3							
Net job creation rate	-14.52%	-9.98%	-15.18%	-1.68%	-6.39%	-22.03%	1.06%
Job creation rate	13.67	8.68	4.89	5.47	1.98	1.14	3.44
Job destruction rate	28.18	18.66	20.07	7.15	8.37	23.17	2.38
Gross job reallocation rate	41.85	27.34	24.96	12.62	10.34	24.30	5.82

Source: Authors' analysis of Maryland quarterly employment data.

TABLE 2-4
Nonmanufacturing

	0-19	20-49	50-99	100-249	250-499	500-999	1000+
1987:3							
Net job creation rate	-0.75%	-1.00%	-2.52%	-1.49%	-0.37%	-0.31%	0.74%
Job creation rate	14.76	8.56	7.69	6.22	7.58	4.21	2.85
Job destruction rate	15.51	9.56	10.21	7.71	7.96	4.53	2.11
Gross job reallocation rate	30.27	18.12	17.89	13.93	15.54	8.74	4.96
1990:3							
Net job creation rate	-4.48%	-3.51%	-1.21%	-3.84%	-5.85%	-1.45%	-0.82%
Job creation rate	13.82	7.52	10.03	5.79	4.15	6.44	1.83
Job destruction rate	18.30	11.04	11.24	9.63	10.00	7.89	2.65
Gross job reallocation rate	32.12	18.56	21.27	15.41	14.15	14.33	4.48
1993:3							
Net job creation rate	-10.52%	-7.41%	-4.49%	-2.18%	-0.64%	-3.50%	-0.75%
Job creation rate	14.19	7.32	6.50	5.73	7.85	7.61	1.22
Job destruction rate	24.71	14.74	10.99	7.91	7.21	11.11	1.87
Gross job reallocation rate	38.90	22.06	17.49	13.64	15.06	18.71	2.99

Source: Authors' analysis of Maryland quarterly employment data.

- The three gross job creation rate observations are *highest* among employing units in the smallest employment-size class of fewer than 20 workers. However, unlike the nation in the 1970s and 1980s, two of Maryland's *lowest* gross job creation rates are not found in the largest employment-size class but in the 500-999 workers size class.[12]

- Our three snapshots of Maryland's gross job destruction rates in 1987:3, 1990:3, and 1993:3 depart from the nation's earlier 1973-88 manufacturing sector experience. Davis, Haltiwanger, and Schuh estimated a 6.8% average gross job destruction rate for manufacturing plants employing 1,000+ workers, which is the *lowest* gross job destruction rate they observed among all the employment-size classes. Maryland suffered a 15.81% gross job destruction rate for the second-largest size class (500-999) in 1987:3, the highest rate among the size classes for that quarter.

- The 1990:3 gross job destruction rates in Table 2-3 strengthen the position of those who warn against giving too much weight to single historical observations of the nation's restructuring of manufacturing activity. Davis, Haltiwanger, and Schuh found a monotonic decline of average gross job destruction rates across employment-size classes. We see here that, during the first quarter of the nation's official 1990-91 recession, Maryland's manufacturing sector absorbed the structural shock with a less uniform pattern of employment-size-class effects. Four of the seven size classes, including the three smallest ones, had virtually identical gross job destruction rates of just under 15%, more than four times higher than the 3.4% job destruction rate for the 1,000+ size class in this quarter.

- The job reallocation rate in the smallest size class increased from 28% in 1987 and 27% in 1990 to 42% in 1993. Table 2-3 shows why this happened among employing units in the 0-19 size class – the gross job destruction rate doubled while the gross job creation rate remained stable between 1987 and 1993.

Figures for Maryland's nonmanufacturing sectors (Table 2-4) differ from those of manufacturing revealed in Table 2-2 and Table 2-3.

- The gross job creation and job destruction rates are uniformly highest in the smallest employment-size class and lowest in the largest size class in each of the three quarterly snapshots. The net job creation rates over the six-year period have been more volatile, particularly in the smaller employment-size classes. Overall, the 21 net job creation rates (seven size classes times three snapshots for each) in Maryland's nonmanufacturing sector fall between a net contraction rate of 10.5% and a net growth rate of 0.7%. In the smallest employment-size class of 0-19 workers the net job creation rate was negative and growing over time, from a net contraction rate of 0.7% in 1987:3 to 10.5% in 1993:3. As in the manufacturing sector of Maryland's economy, this pattern results from a growing gross job destruction rate coupled with a stable gross job creation rate. The cross-section of job reallocation rates across the size classes, which range from 2.9% to 38.9%, is similar in many respects to the manufacturing sector rates that appear in Table 2-3.

From a manufacturing versus nonmanufacturing job flows perspective alone, there is no basis for praising one part of Maryland's business community and damning another. With the single exception of the downsizing hit that occurred in the largest manufacturing size class in 1987, the patterns of gross job creation and gross job destruction, and the derivative concepts of gross job reallocation and net job creation, are strikingly similar in the two sectors. However, it should be noted that this statement refers to a similarity of flow rates; differences in the number of employing units in each of the employment-size-class cells in the manufacturing and nonmanufacturing sectors would have to be considered to properly interpret the ramifications of the differences that have been highlighted. Also, up to this point we have focused on *job* flows. A complementary perspective concentrating on *worker* flows offers additional insights.

> **We focus on three measures of worker flows: (1) hires, (2) exits, and (3) total turnover.**

Worker flows

The remainder of this paper departs from the manufacturing sector and employment-size class constraints adopted in the previous section to offer a direct comparison with Davis and Haltiwanger's results. We take advantage of the individual employee records in our database to reveal the basic attributes of worker flows that interacted with the job dynamics documented in Tables 2-3 and 2-4.

Relying on snapshot counts of incumbent workers alone, job reallocation rate calculations have offered valuable insights about the heterogeneity that exists among firms within an industry and among regions. Other researchers, including Davis and Haltiwanger (1994), Eberts and Montgomery (1994), and Grey (1994), have recognized and dealt conceptually with the bounds that job reallocation places on worker opportunities to change employer affiliation or employment status. Our Maryland database contains both job counts and employee identifiers, which means that we are able to explore *worker* flows within the employment-size classes. We have chosen to focus on three measures of worker flows: (1) *hires,* (2) *exits,* and (3) *total turnover*.

The quarterly reports filed by Maryland's employers identify every worker who was paid in each three-month period. This means that a series of three consecu-

TABLE 2-5A
Distribution of hires, exits, and turnover by size class

	0-4	5-49	50-99	100-249	250-999	1000+
1987:3						
Hires	6.15%	32.27%	12.38%	14.79%	18.88%	15.53%
Exits	6.26	32.42	12.92	15.18	19.06	14.17
Turnover	6.21	32.35	12.65	14.99	18.97	14.83
Employment	6.28	25.68	9.51	12.83	18.07	27.62
1990:3						
Hires	6.70%	32.44%	12.94%	14.53%	17.91%	15.50%
Exits	7.03	33.43	12.76	14.19	17.73	14.86
Turnover	6.87	32.97	12.84	14.35	17.81	15.15
Employment	6.63	25.50	9.40	12.38	16.60	29.49
1993:3						
Hires	6.68%	31.28%	11.97%	15.21%	18.49%	16.36%
Exits	6.53	31.24	11.89	15.33	17.81	17.21
Turnover	6.61	31.26	11.93	15.28	17.29	16.79
Employment	6.38	24.40	9.08	13.03	16.96	30.16

Source: Authors' analysis of Maryland quarterly employment data.

tive quarters of data can be used to determine whether a worker in the second, or middle, of the three quarters appears for the first or last time in the series. A worker who appears in the second but not in the first quarter of the series is defined as a hire. A worker who appears in the second but not in the third quarter of the series is defined as an exit. Total turnover is the sum of hires and exits. We have not attempted to look beyond this nine-month interval to determine whether a worker identified as a hire ever worked for the employing unit before, or whether what we call an exit subsequently becomes a recall beyond the one quarter that has been checked.

Tables 2-5A and **2-5B** present our findings from the three snapshots taken – 1987:3, 1990:3, and 1993:3. Robust economic prosperity reigned in Maryland in 1987, although the direct and ripple effects of defense sector cutbacks had already begun. The second observation was taken during what has been officially designated as the beginning quarter of the 1990-91 U.S. recession. The third observation was made a full year after the end of the national recession, but in a state that is now known to have lagged the nation in economic recovery. Nevertheless, three distinct cyclical segments are represented here.

Each of the three panels in Table 2-5A contains a line showing the distribution of total employment by employment-size class. These distributions remained essentially constant over the six-year reference period. Micro-employing units (those with fewer than five paid workers) accounted for only 6% of Maryland's covered

TABLE 2-5B
Relative distribution of hires, exits, and turnover by size class

	0-4	5-49	50-99	100-249	250-999	1000+
1987:3						
Hires	0.98	1.26	1.30	1.15	1.04	0.56
Exits	1.00	1.26	1.36	1.18	1.05	0.51
Turnover	0.99	1.26	1.33	1.17	1.05	0.53
1990:3						
Hires	1.01	1.27	1.38	1.17	1.08	0.53
Exits	1.06	1.31	1.36	1.15	1.07	0.50
Turnover	1.04	1.29	1.37	1.16	1.07	0.51
1993:3						
Hires	1.05	1.28	1.32	1.17	1.09	0.54
Exits	1.02	1.28	1.31	1.18	1.05	0.57
Turnover	1.04	1.28	1.31	1.17	1.02	0.56

Source: Authors' analysis of Maryland quarterly employment data.

employment, while the largest employing units of 1,000+ workers accounted for approximately 30% of total employment. These figures can be placed in the context of the number of reporting employing units in each size class by referring back to Table 2-1, which shows that over 55% of the employing units fall in the micro-business size class of fewer than five paid workers and that only 0.2% of the reporting business units fall in the 1,000+ size class.

The distribution of hire shares by employment-size class[13] – the first line in each of the three panels of Table 2-5A – is stable over the six-year period. The smallest micro-businesses have a hire share of about 6%, which is the same as their share of total employment. This relationship is repeated in the 250-999 size class, where the six observations (two shares calculated three times) cluster between 17% and 19%. This proportionality contrasts with a hire share of 16% in the 1,000+ size class or barely over half the employment share of that size class, which ranges between 28% and 30% in the three observations. This low hire share is made up by the mid-range employment-size classes.

The relationships described in the previous paragraph can be seen more clearly by looking at Table 2-5B, where each size class cell in the hires, exits, and total turnover lines of Table 2-5A is divided by its corresponding employment share. In Table 2-5B, any figure greater than one indicates that the employment-size class contributed more than its expected share of the activity in question (hires, exits, or total turnover). This assumes that the "expected" share of each activity for a particular employment-size class is its share of total employment – an expectation that many small business scholars would not necessarily share. This approach is adopted for expository purposes only; it provides an easily understood way to describe the nature of employment dynamics in Maryland.

The ratios in Table 2-5B offer compelling evidence that Maryland's micro-businesses contribute to hires, exits, and turnover in virtually identical shares to their total employment. All of the nine ratios for this size class (three ratios calculated three times) cluster between values of 0.98 and 1.06. A similar consistency, but at ratios half this level, is found within the largest size class of 1000+ workers – here, the hire, exit, and turnover rates as a percentage of the size class's share of statewide employment range between 0.50 and 0.57.

The "action" in worker flows is in the mid-range of the employment-size class categories – the three size classes (5-49, 50-99, and 100-249 workers) exhibit hire, exit, and turnover ratios ranging from a low of 1.15 to a high of 1.38. These are the Maryland businesses that are contributing more than their "expected" share of the worker flow action. There has been no significant change in the size class pattern of any of these worker flow measures over the six-year period 1987-93. The approximate balance of hire and exit rate ratios within each size class documents the heterogeneity of actions taken by individual workers and business managers who are reflected in each series of year/quarter and size class cells.

Another way to look at the worker flow issue is to examine hire and exit rates by employment-size class and over time. **Table 2-6** lists hire and exit rates calculated by identifying the percentage of all occupied positions reported by employing units assigned to the employment-size class that satisfy the definition of a hire or an exit as these were defined earlier in this paper.[14] Consistent with the patterns identified in Tables 2-5A and 2-5B, the highest hire and exit rates occurred in the mid-range size classes – approximately one out of every four workers reported as working for an employing unit in the four size classes covering 5-999 workers in the 1987 and 1990 third-quarter snapshots did not have the same business affiliation in the previous quarter (hires) or in the subsequent quarter (exits). Across *all* size classes there has been a uniform decline in both hire and exit rates between 1987-90 and 1993. This can be seen by comparing the first two lines in both the upper (hires) and lower (exits) panels of Table 2-6 with the third line of each panel. Two quite different interpretations can be given to this pervasive change: (1) structural corrections made before 1993:3, some of which appear in the 1987 and 1990 data, have reduced the need for sustained worker flows of the same magnitude; and (2) Maryland's slow emergence from the 1990-91 national recession has not created opportunities and incentives to continue the previous level of reallocation. These are not mutually exclusive explanations; each contributes to our understanding of the state's employment dynamics.

TABLE 2-6
Hiring and exit rates by firm size

	0-4	5-49	50-99	100-249	250-999	1000+
Hiring rates						
1987:3	19.37%	24.83%	25.72%	22.77%	20.63%	11.11%
1990:3	18.61	23.44	25.35	21.62	19.87	9.68
1993:3	14.42	17.65	18.16	16.08	15.02	7.47
Exit rates						
1987:3	20.59%	26.08%	28.06%	24.44%	21.78%	10.59%
1990:3	22.55	27.90	28.87	24.40	22.72	10.72
1993:3	14.68	18.36	18.79	16.89	15.07	8.19

Source: Authors' analysis of Maryland quarterly employment data.

Continuity of a worker's employer affiliation

There has been a flurry of controversy about whether fundamental changes in average job tenure have occurred in the United States.[15] Farber (1992, 6) concludes that "simply put, none of the evidence presented here supports [the] popular view that long-term jobs are disappearing or even becoming less common in the United States." Similarly, Diebold, Neumark, and Polsky (1994, 17) conclude that "in our view, the general conclusion to emerge from our study is the approximate *stability* of aggregate job retention rates over the 1980s and early 1990s, in contrast to pronounced shifts in the wage distribution."

Here, we take advantage of the continuous series of Maryland's quarterly wage records from mid-1985 into 1992 to investigate the job tenure issue from an employment-size-class vantage point. First, we assigned all employing units that reported in 1985:3 to an employment-size class. Then we identified all hires by these employing units in this quarter and tracked the length of their continued affiliation with this employing unit for a maximum of 81 months (27 quarters).[16] Affiliations that were terminated during the base-period quarter (1985:3) are omitted from Figures 2-1A and 2-1B; these would be simultaneous hires and exits because these workers both arrived and departed from an employing unit in the same reference quarter.

Figures 2-1A and **2-1B** present the employment-size class features of the analysis. Figure 2-1A shows the share of each recorded length of employer affiliation that is contributed by employing units of a particular size. The seven employment-size classes that appear in the previous tables have been reduced to three size classes – 0-49, 50-249, and 250+ workers – so the pattern is easier to see.

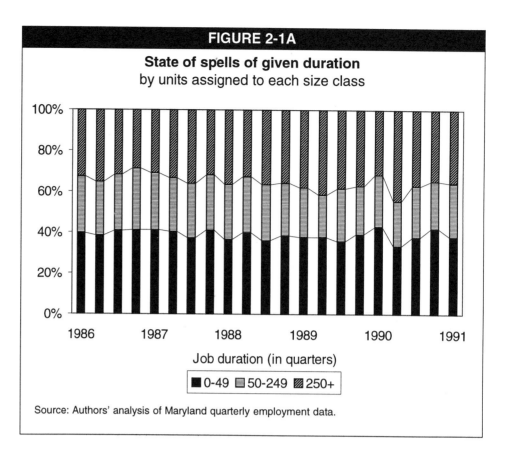

FIGURE 2-1A

State of spells of given duration
by units assigned to each size class

Job duration (in quarters)

■ 0-49 ▤ 50-249 ▨ 250+

Source: Authors' analysis of Maryland quarterly employment data.

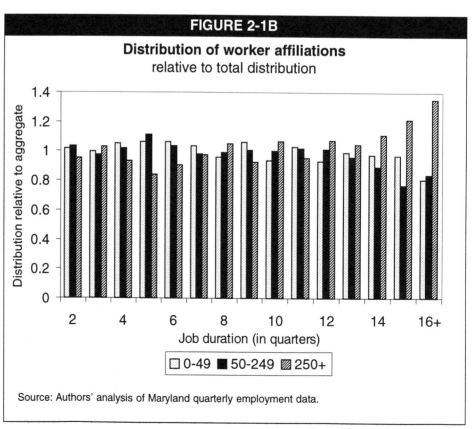

FIGURE 2-1B

Distribution of worker affiliations
relative to total distribution

Job duration (in quarters)

▥ 0-49 ■ 50-249 ▨ 250+

Source: Authors' analysis of Maryland quarterly employment data.

Figure 2-1A shows that employing units in the three size classes contributed in roughly equal shares to the shorter lengths of continuous employer affiliation, which appear on the left side of the figure, but that the employing units assigned to the largest employment-size class account for a much larger percentage of the longer affiliations, including the truncated ones that had not been severed by the end of the observation period.

The size class mix reflected in quarters beginning with the 19th in Figure 2-1A, which are recession and post-recession quarters, suggests that workers affiliated with smaller employing units in 1985:3[17] were less affected than their larger counterparts by the structural dynamics that occurred during and immediately after the recession of the early 1990s.[18] Factors that contribute to either employing unit or worker hazard rates, or to both, produce the pattern that appears in Figure 2-1A. Figure 2-1B looks at the length of worker affiliations by employment-size class from a different perspective. Here, each vertical bar represents a ratio calculated as a particular size class's share of completed employing unit affiliation spells of the designated length[19] divided by that quarter's share of the total number of observed exits (or truncated continuing affiliation spells). This ratio will have a value of 1.0 when a size class contributes to exit events in a reference quarter in the same proportion as that quarter's share of the total number of exit events observed. A ratio value of less than 1.0 signals that the employing units assigned to that employment-size class are "underrepresented" in completed affiliation spells of that length; a ratio larger than 1.0 indicates "overrepresentation."

Figure 2-1B shows that employing units assigned to the smallest of the three size classes (0-49 workers) are overrepresented in the shorter lengths of affiliation – seven out of the 10 durations of 11 quarters or less – and underrepresented in the longer durations – four out of the five durations of 12 or more quarters. The ratio difference is largest in the truncated continuing affiliation category of 16+ quarters, where the dominance of larger employing units is most apparent.[20]

The length of employing unit affiliation data presented in this section complement and reinforce the findings that appeared in the previous sections on gross job creation, gross job destruction, job reallocation, net job creation, hires, exits, and turnover. We have not attempted to identify employing units that stopped filing quarterly earnings reports, which would be one step toward revealing the relative importance of employer "deaths," mass layoffs, individual terminations, and voluntary departure of workers as explanations for the size-class patterns that were found.

Employing units assigned to the smallest of the three size classes are overrepresented in the shorter lengths of affiliation.

The size-class distribution of average quarterly earnings level

The final component of our analysis of recent small business employment dynamics in Maryland looks at the presence of smaller employing units in a 1987:3 cross-section distribution of average quarterly earnings level by employment-size class, and then investigates whether and how this pattern changed in two subsequent observations (1990:3 and 1993:3). Each average quarterly earnings figure is calculated by dividing an employing unit's total reported earnings amount for all covered workers in a reference quarter by the number of workers reported.[21] The interpretation of the vertical axes in Figures **2-2A**, **2-2B**, and **2-2C** is the same as the explanation given above for Figure 2-1B – each ratio compares a size class to its "expected," or weighted, share of observations at a particular average quarterly earnings level. Again, a ratio of 1.0 indicates that the employing units in a size class are represented at that point on the average quarterly earnings distribution in the same proportion as that average quarterly earnings level's share of all average quarterly earnings observations (i.e., the total distribution). The "overrepresented" and "underrepresented" definitions remain as before.

Figure 2-2A is based on 1987:3 Maryland employing unit reports of employee earnings. Figure 2-2B is for 1990:3, and Figure 2-2C is for 1993:3. This break-

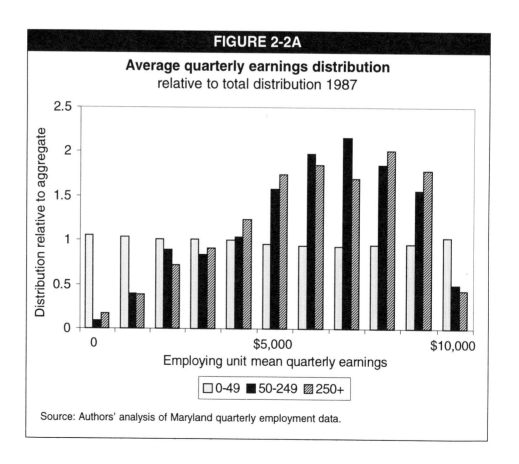

FIGURE 2-2A

Average quarterly earnings distribution
relative to total distribution 1987

0-49 ■ 50-249 ▨ 250+

Source: Authors' analysis of Maryland quarterly employment data.

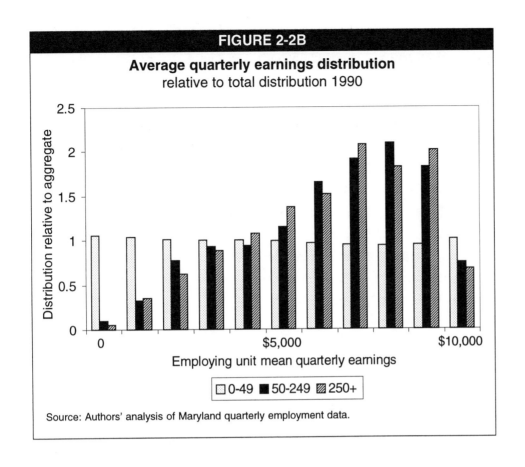

FIGURE 2-2B

Average quarterly earnings distribution
relative to total distribution 1990

Distribution relative to aggregate

Employing unit mean quarterly earnings

☐ 0-49 ■ 50-249 ▨ 250+

Source: Authors' analysis of Maryland quarterly employment data.

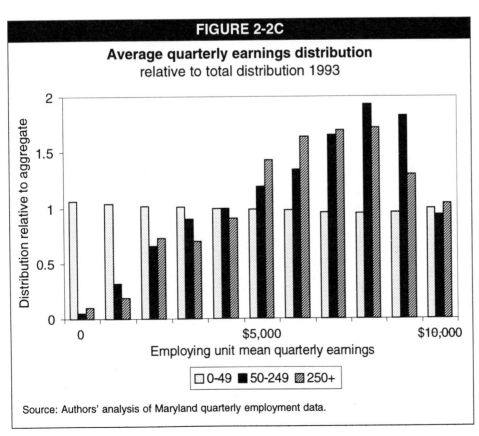

FIGURE 2-2C

Average quarterly earnings distribution
relative to total distribution 1993

Distribution relative to aggregate

Employing unit mean quarterly earnings

☐ 0-49 ■ 50-249 ▨ 250+

Source: Authors' analysis of Maryland quarterly employment data.

down illustrates changes over time in the size-class distributions of average quarterly earnings levels. The employing units assigned to the smallest employment-size class (0-49 workers) in 1987:3 dominate the average quarterly earnings levels of less than $4,000 and $10,000+.[22] The observed dominance of small employing units in the highest average quarterly earnings category reflects the limited number of production and support-staff members within these businesses, whose modest earnings would offset high management and technical staff salaries.

Figures 2-2B and 2-2C reveal easily seen changes in size-class representation at the higher earnings levels. In the highest open-ended category of $10,000+ the employing units in the larger size classes have closed the gap between with their smaller counterparts observed in the 1987:3 data. The monotonic decline in size-class appearance in the $7,000 and above categories in the 1987:3 data has dissolved into a less well defined pattern by 1993:3.

We conclude that there has not been much change in the distribution of average quarterly earnings among small employing units over the six-year observation period 1987-93. A fundamental reason for this, of course, is that by definition there are not many workers within each reporting employing unit whose earnings level and relative standing can change in a short period of time.

CONCLUSION

Two goals have been pursued here. First, we have provided a bare-bones introduction to the insights of other researchers about small business employment dynamics that burst onto the scene in 1994 in somewhat inaccessible specialized journals, formal working papers, and manuscripts presented at recent international conferences. And second, we have added new findings based on one state's quarterly earnings data covering the period 1985-93.

Our own analysis generally confirms and updates what others have said about the manufacturing sector, but we have also complemented these findings with comparable data for the nonmanufacturing sector. Fundamental similarities of small business employment dynamics in these two components of the economy have been documented, at least for Maryland since the mid-1980s. In particular, we find the following:

- New and expanding small[23] businesses appear to create new jobs at a higher rate than their larger[24] counterparts, but this relationship is sensitive to cyclical forces.

- Shrinking and dying small businesses exhibit a higher rate of job destruction than their larger counterparts, and this pattern also is affected by cyclical events.

- The combined effect of these creative and destructive forces reveals a much more distinct moving target of employment opportunity within the small business sector than in larger enterprises.

- With respect to the bottom line issue of net job creation, this database reveals no apparent pattern with respect to business size class.

- Average employee job tenure is substantially longer for larger businesses.

- Average quarterly earnings are greater in large than small firms.

It is hoped that, at this point, the reader will have a more informed appreciation of the complexities of small business employment dynamics. At a minimum, he or she will probably be more cautious about accepting standalone assertions about the small business sector's role in the economy. Just as there is no perfect data source, there is no "representative" observation period. The new findings reported here rest on a platform of prior knowledge, and perhaps these findings can serve as a new platform on which to base further research.

With respect to the bottom line issue of net job creation, this database reveals no apparent pattern with respect to business size class.

DATA APPENDIX

Data structure

These are confidential records. The agreement between the University of Baltimore and Maryland's Department of Economic and Employment Development specifies the uses that can be made of these data and stipulates that the identities of individuals and firms cannot be revealed to the public. The data are encrypted upon arrival and then stored and processed in a secure facility. Staff members who have access to the data sign an oath indicating their awareness of the law's requirements and their personal intention to abide by these stipulations

The micro records used in this paper represent both single establishment firms, multiple establishment firms that report each of the subordinate establishment's information separately, and multiple establishment firms that combine all of the subordinate unit information into a single entity. This raises issues about the differences between firms and establishments and the consequences of firm changes in the employer identification number. Note, however, that a business can be "born" and "die" without ever having employed anyone; and an employer identification number can be recycled. Neither of these attributes of the database affects the findings that are reported here. Many of these issues are clearly addressed in Anderson and Meyer (1994) and have also been addressed in Lane, Isaac, and Stevens (1993). Errors that might arise from late reporting are minimized by acquiring each quarter of Maryland data twice: when it first becomes available three months after the end of the reference quarter, and then again two quarters later. Nonreporting and erroneous reporting of individual employee's affiliations do affect the estimates that are reported here. However, these administrative records are used in the day-to-day management of the state's unemployment compensation program. This results in a high rate of compliance, as is the case in any mandatory reporting situation that involves recurring and unpredictable accessing of the records for eligibility and payment determination purposes. Late reporting occurs because of the quarterly timing of required submission. This does not affect the archival records because they are routinely updated to reflect such cases.

It is important to distinguish between the substantial progress that has been made through the BLS-SESAs cooperative agreements to achieve establishment-level employment counts and the not-yet-addressed issue of requiring establishment-level reporting of individual employee affiliations. The latter is required for an accurate tracing of employee flows among establishments within larger legal business entities.

First quarter data reflect accumulated "noneconomic" changes that can be traced to such origins as industry coding changes that occurred during the most recent of the three-year recurring updates of employer-specific standard industrial classification codes; changes associated with predecessor and successor linkages of unemployment compensation account identification codes; and routine purging practices for business entities that have not self-described themselves as having "died" but which have not reported actual employee earnings for multiple sequential quarters. The fourth-quarter data reflect cyclically sensitive seasonal factors (holiday consumer spending and related hiring practices) and end-of-year legal/accounting transactions that would be expected to be sensitive to tax law and regulatory changes.

Construction of dataset

We are primarily interested in this paper in looking at employment spells that exist for at least a quarter. We therefore define people as being employed for a full quarter by making quarter-to-quarter matches of employer/employee pairs for three consecutive quarters. We assume that a worker who shows up as working for the same employer for three consecutive quarters is employed for the entire middle quarter. We define hires as people who were not with the firm in the preceding quarter (in the above definition) but who were there in the current quarter; we define exits analogously (this requires five quarters of data). The coding error rate of Social Security numbers is 0.003%, which will result in incorrect identification of hires and exits in a commensurate number of cases.

Representativeness

Appendix Table 1 compares the industrial distribution of employment in Maryland to the nation's industry mix of employment in 1990 and as projected by the Bureau of Labor Statistics for the year 2005. Maryland's employment mix is more like that projected for the turn of the century, which makes the analysis reported here of particular interest from a policy importance and replication standpoint. In particular, it is evident that the move from manufacturing to non-manufacturing, which has been so marked in the 1980s, is projected to continue into the next century. This would suggest that studies that focus only on the manufacturing sector will be of less interest to policy makers than studies that provide data on every sector of the economy.

APPENDIX TABLE 1
Employment by sector

	US(1990)	US(2005)	Maryland
Agriculture, mining, construction	8.1 %	7.2%	9.9%
Manufacturing	16.9	13.6	10.4
Transportation, communication	5.2	4.9	5.7
Wholesale, retail trade	22.3	23.6	27.5
Finance, insurance, real estate	6.0	6.0	6.5
Services	24.5	28.8	33.1
Government	16.3	15.9	6.9

Source: *Monthly Labor Review* (November 1991) (moderate); authors' tabulations.

ENDNOTES

1. *Workforce Development Strategies*, Vol. 6, No. 10 (March 1995), p. 8.

2. One symposium, titled "Small Business in the U.S. Economy," containing six articles, appeared in *Business Economics*, Vol. 29, No. 3 (July 1994), pp. 7-42. Another symposium on this topic was slated to appear in the journal *Small Business Economics*. One of three volumes summarizing *The OECD Jobs Study: Evidence and Explanations, Part 1 – Labour Market Trends and Underlying Forces of Change* (Paris: Organization for Economic Cooperation and Development, 1994), includes a section titled *Job Creation and Job Destruction* (pp. 16-18). More detailed findings and analytical discussion appear in Alex Grey, "Job Gains and Job Losses: Recent Literature and Trends," Working Paper Series No. 1, *OECD Jobs Study* (Paris: OECD, 1994, p. 76). Two recent international conferences hosted by different German research institutes investigated small business employment dynamics: the WZB convened a December 1994 conference on the theme "The Flow Approach to Labour Market Analysis"; the ZEW followed with a January 1995 conference focusing on the "Dynamics of Employment and Industry Evolution." The National Bureau of Economic Research Conference on Research in Income and Wealth hosted a two-day session in December 1994 on "Labor Statistics Measurement Issues." Insights from these documents are reflected throughout this paper.

3. Alex Grey, op cit, *Annex A: Sources, Definitions and Methods of Data Collection on Job Gains and Job Losses*, pp. 25-37, describes the basic features of major datasets covering Canada, Denmark, Finland, France, Germany, Italy, New Zealand, Norway, Sweden, the United Kingdom, and the United States.

4. The symposium articles scheduled to appear at the time of this writing in "Small Business Economics" offer a potpourri of views on the strengths and weaknesses of U.S. data sources for conducting research on small business employment dynamics.

5. A detailed description of this data source appears in an appendix to this paper.

6. Davis and Haltiwanger (1994), Eberts and Montgomery (1994), and Grey (1994) provide excellent up-to-date reviews of the literature. This section draws heavily from each of these sources and presents only a few highlights from sophisticated studies of small business employment dynamics.

7. J. Baldwin and G. Picot, "Employment Generation by Small Producers in the Canadian Manufacturing Sector," in the journal *Small Business Economics*.

8. G. Picot, J. Baldwin, and R. Duprey (1994), *Have Small Firms Created a Disproportionate Share of New Jobs in Canada? A Reassessment of the Facts*.

9. The Office of Labor Market Analysis and Information in Maryland's Department of Economic and Employment Development processes a *multiple worksite report* as a supplement to the quarterly contribution and wage report for multi-establishment *employing units* that are known to the department. The comprehensiveness of this refinement has increased in recent years, but this program identifies only the establishment-specific average employment *level* for each of the three months in the reference quarter. The identities of workers who are affiliated with each establishment are not revealed, thus precluding a direct analysis of *worker* flows at the establishment level for these multi-establishment enterprises.

10. This index of job quality simply records the number of occupied positions at two or more points in time. If later observations detect a larger number of incumbent employees, then employment opportunity can be said to have increased; the opposite would be true if the later count is lower than the base-period figure. Nothing is revealed about any changes over time in the skill requirements, working conditions, labor-management relations, or compensation associated with these snapshot counts of job incumbents.

11. Caution is advised when comparing Table 2-2 and Table 2-3 figures. Davis, Haltiwanger, and Schuh used the Census Longitudinal Research Datafile of manufacturing establishments, while we use Maryland Department of Economic and Employment Development quarterly wage records and ES-202 data that combine job and worker data elements. Our files include both production plants and management headquarters activities. Table 2-4 presents new findings for the nonmanufacturing sector of Maryland's economy. The cells in this table are directly comparable to the manufacturing cells in Table 2-3.

12. This difference is consistent with what would be expected, given our previous warning, that the largest employment-size class of 1,000+ workers is a heterogeneous combination of very large single-establishment businesses and multi-establishment *employing units* that combine the employment of more than one smaller business unit into a single large reporting entity. This causes an averaging of *gross job creation* behaviors by *employing units* that Davis, Haltiwanger, and Schuh have assigned to different employment-size classes using the Longitudinal Research Datafile.

13. Each share figure that appears in Table 2-5A is a particular cell's count as a percentage of the *row* total. For example, the 1987:3 hires share figure of 6.15% for the size class 0-4 workers indicates that 6% of *all* Maryland hires that were identified in the third quarter 1987 data were initiated by employing units assigned to the smallest micro-business size class.

14. Employers report earnings for each worker who was paid during a reference quarter. This means that there may be multiple sequential incumbents in a single "position," as this term is normally understood. This is why measurement of worker flows differs from that of job flows, where the latter concept reflects only aggregate (employer-specific) changes over time in the number of occupied positions reported (i.e., without respect to whether the incumbent is a new, continuing, or subsequently departed worker). Heterogeneity in worker flows exists within employing units (i.e., among positions), among employing units within an industry, within each of the diverse parts of the state, and among these regions.

15. See F.X. Diebold, D. Neumark, and D. Polsky, 1994, *Job Stability in the United States*, Working Paper No. 4859, Cambridge, Mass.: National Bureau of Economic Research, and H.S. Farber, 1994, "Are Lifetime Jobs Disappearing? Job Duration in the United States: 1973-1993," prepared for a conference on research in income and wealth session, titled *Labor Statistics Measurement Issues*. Cambridge, Mass.: National Bureau of Economic Research.

16. The accuracy of this method of measuring continuity of employer affiliation depends upon the accurate reporting of each worker's Social Security number *every* quarter, because any error creates a false break in the continuous series. Also, the ownership issue arises again. A worker who continues an unbroken string of quarters worked at the same establishment will be incorrectly defined as a *mover* if a change of ownership results in the worker's earnings being reported under a new Unemployment Insurance Employer Account Number. Each of these sources of error *lowers* the estimated length of continuous *job* affiliation. The late 1980s was a period of intense acquisition and merger activity, so the ownership bias should not be ignored.

17. We have not attempted to separate worker affiliations that ended because the entire employing unit stopped reporting from those associated with "mass" layoffs and others that might be characterized as individual events. This refinement will be carried out in future research using this database. Also, the size class assignment made here is a one-time designation based on 1985:4 employment levels. Cross-boundary reclassification opportunities over the observation period have not been examined.

18. Caution is urged to avoid overstating the importance of this relationship from an actionability standpoint. First, all of the completed affiliation spells of 19 or more quarters, and the spells that are truncated in quarter 27, are in the tail of the distribution of all observed affiliation spells that began as a Maryland hire in 1985:3. Most of the completed spells in *all* three of the employment-size classes shown had ended before the 1990 recession began. And, second, the larger employing units contribute many more workers to any quarter's reservoir of *potential* candidates for *exit* during that reference period. This means that the role of large employing units in the cyclical adjustment process is magnified in Figure 2-1A.

19. Spell lengths of two through 15 quarters are completed affiliations, but the 16+ category includes continuing affiliations that are truncated at the end of the 81-month observation period. This 16+ category was selected because there are relatively few continuing affiliations longer than four years in this population of 1985:3 hires.

20. This is simply another way of showing the same relationship that appears in Figure 2-1A.

21. This very rough measure of earnings differences across employment-size classes will be refined in our future research to define, derive, and analyze multiple measures of earnings distributions, and changes in these distributions, within reporting employing units assigned to different employment-size classes. These earnings distribution issues will be examined in the context of boundary crossing issues, age of the employing unit, and the job and worker flow measures used here.

22. The ratio values for the smallest employment-size class of 0-49 workers are always close to 1.0 because the number of employing units assigned to this size class far exceeds that in the two larger size classes. The effects of weighting observations are more apparent in the larger size classes in both Figures 2-1 and 2-2.

23. Fewer than 50 employees.

24. More than 250 employees.

BIBLIOGRAPHY

Baldwin J., and G. Picot. "Employment Generation by Small Producers in the Canadian Manufacturing Sector." *Small Business Economics*, forthcoming.

Berney, R.E., and B.D. Phillips. 1994. *Small Business and Job Creation – An Update.* Washington, D.C.: U.S. Department of Commerce, Office of Advocacy, Small Business Administration.

Birch, D. L. 1979. *The Job Generation Process.* Cambridge, Mass.: MIT Program on Neighborhood and Regional Change.

Burgess, S., J. Lane, and D. Stevens. 1994. *Job Flows and Worker Flows Over the Life-Cycle of a Firm.* Berlin, Germany: WZB.

Davis, S.J., and J. Haltiwanger. 1990. "Gross Job Creation and Destruction: Microeconomic Evidence and Macroeconomic Implications." *National Bureau of Economic Research, Macroeconomics Annual*, Vol. 5, pp. 123-68.

Davis, S.J., and J. Haltiwanger. 1992. "Gross Job Creation, Gross Job Destruction, and Employment Reallocation." *Quarterly Journal of Economics*, Vol. 107, No. 3, pp. 819-64.

Davis, S.J., and J. Haltiwanger. 1994. *Measuring Gross Worker and Job Flows.* Prepared for NBER Conference on Research in Income and Wealth: Labor Statistics Measurement Issues, December 15. Cambridge, Mass.: National Bureau of Economic Research.

Davis, S.J., J. Haltiwanger, and S. Schuh. 1994. "Small Business and Job Creation: Dissecting the Myth and Reassessing the Facts." *Business Economics*, Vol. 29, No. 3, pp. 13-21.

Dennis, W.J. Jr., B.D. Phillips, and E. Starr. 1994. "Small Business Job Creation: The Findings and Their Critics." *Business Economics*, Vol. 29, No. 3, pp. 23-30.

Diebold, F.X., D. Neumark, and D. Polsky. 1994. *Job Stability in the United States.* Working Paper No. 4859. Cambridge, Mass.: National Bureau of Economic Research.

Duncan, J.W., and D.P. Handler. 1994. "The Misunderstood Role of Small Business." *Business Economics*, Vol. 29, No. 3, pp. 7-12.

Dunne, T., M. Roberts, and L. Samuelson. 1989. "Plant Turnover and Gross Employment Flows in the U.S. Manufacturing Sector." *Journal of Labor Economics*, Vol. 7, No. 1, pp. 48-71.

Eberts, R.W., and E.B. Montgomery. 1994. "Employment Creation and Destruction: An Analytical Review." *Economic Review*. Cleveland, Ohio: Federal Reserve Bank of Cleveland, Vol. 30, No. 3, pp. 14-26.

Farber, H.S. 1994. "Are Lifetime Jobs Disappearing? Job Duration in the United States: 1973- 1993." Prepared for NBER Conference on Research in Income and Wealth: Labor Statistics Measurement Issues, December 15. Cambridge, Mass.: National Bureau of Economic Research.

Gottschalk, P., and R. Moffitt. 1994. "The Growth of Earnings Instability in the U.S. Labor Market," *Brookings Papers on Economic Activity*, Vol. 2, pp. 217-54.

Grey, A. 1994. *Job Gains and Job Losses: Recent Literature and Trends.* Working Paper Series No. 1. Paris, France: Organization for Economic Cooperation and Development.

Harrison, B. 1994. *Lean and Mean: The Changing Landscape of Corporate Power in the Age of Flexibility*, New York, N.Y.: Basic Books.

Lane, J., and D. Stevens. 1995. "Work, Family, and Welfare History; Work and Welfare Outcomes." *American Economic Review*, Vol. 85, No. 3.

Leonard, J.S. 1987. "In the Wrong Place at the Wrong Time: The Extent of Frictional and Structural Unemployment." In K. Lang and J. Leonard, eds., *Unemployment and the Structure of Labor Markets*. New York, N.Y.: Basil Blackwell.

Organization for Economic Cooperation and Development. 1994. *The OECD Jobs Study: Evidence and Explanations, Part I – Labour Market Trends and Underlying Forces of Change.* Paris, France: OECD.

Picot, G., J. Baldwin, and R. Duprey. 1994. *Have Small Firms Created a Disproportionate Share of New Jobs in Canada? A Reassessment of the Facts.*

White, S., and J.D. Osterman. 1991. "Is Employment Growth Really Coming From Small Establishments?" *Economic Development Quarterly*, Vol. 5, No. 3, pp. 241-57.

White, S., J.F. Zipp, W.F. McMahon, P.D. Reynolds, J.D. Osterman, and L.S. Binkley. 1990. "ES202: The Data Base for Local Employment Analysis." *Economic Development Quarterly*, Vol. 4, No. 3, pp. 240-53.

Workforce Development Strategies. 1995. Vol. 6, No. 10, p. 8.

RECENT EPI BOOKS

THE STATE OF WORKING AMERICA 1996-97
by Lawrence Mishel, Jared Bernstein, & John Schmitt
0-7656-0024-2 (paper) $24.95
0-7656-0221-0 (cloth) $55.00

GETTING PRICES RIGHT
The Debate Over the Consumer Price Index
edited by Dean Baker
0-7656-0222-9 (paper) $19.95
0-7656-0221-0 (cloth) $50.95

RISKY BUSINESS
Private Management of Public Schools
by Craig E. Richards, Rima Shore, &Max B. Sawicky
0-944826-68-7 (paper) $19.95

RECLAIMING PROSPERITY: A Blueprint for
Progressive Economic Reform
edited by Todd Schafer & Jeff Faux
Preface by Lester Thurow
1-56324-769-0 (paper) $19.95
1-56324-768-2 (cloth) $62.50

**THE MACROECONOMICS OF SAVING,
FINANCE, AND INVESTMENT**
edited by Robert Pollin
0-472-10787-9 (cloth) $52.00

SCHOOL CHOICE
Examining the Evidence
edited by Edith Rasell & Richard Rothstein
0-944826-57-1 (paper) $17.95

U.S. TRADE POLICY AND GLOBAL GROWTH
New Directions in the International Economy
edited by Robert A. Blecker
1-56324-531-1 (paper) $22.95
1-56324-530-2 (cloth) $52.50

BEWARE THE U.S. MODEL
Jobs & Wages in a Deregulated Economy
edited by Lawrence Mishel & John Schmitt
0-944826-58-X (paper) $24.95

THE NEW AMERICAN WORKPLACE: Transforming
Work Systems in the United States
by Eileen Appelbaum & Rosemary Batt
0-87332-828-0 (paper) $18.95
0-87332-827-2 (cloth) $45.00

UNIONS AND ECONOMIC COMPETITIVENESS
edited by Lawrence Mishel & Paula B. Voos
0-87332-828-0 (paper) $20.95
0-87332-827-2 (cloth) $46.95

HOW TO ORDER

All orders for EPI books, studies, working papers, and briefing papers should be addressed to:

EPI Publications
1660 L Street, NW, Suite 1200, Washington, D.C. 20036

or call: **800-EPI-4844** (202-331-5510 in Washington area)

Orders can be faxed to: **(202) 775-0819.**

EPI will send a complete catalog of all publications. Discounts are available to libraries and bookstores and for quantity sales.

EPI's website contains executive summaries and introductions to recent EPI books and studies. Publications can be ordered from the website as well. The address is:

http://www.epinet.org

RECENT EPI STUDIES

ABOUT EPI

The Economic Policy Institute was founded in 1986 to widen the debate about policies to achieve healthy economic growth, prosperity, and opportunity in the difficult new era America has entered.

Today, America's economy is threatened by slow growth and increasing inequality. Expanding global competition, changes in the nature of work, and rapid technological advances are altering economic reality. Yet many of our policies, attitudes, and institutions are based on assumptions that no longer reflect real world conditions.

Central to the Economic Policy Institute's search for solutions is the exploration of policies that encourage every segment of the American economy (business, labor, government, universities, voluntary organizations, etc.) to work cooperatively to raise productivity and living standards for all Americans. Such an undertaking involves a challenge to conventional views of market behavior and a revival of a cooperative relationship between the public and private sectors.

With the support of leaders from labor, business, and the foundation world, the Institute has sponsored research and public discussion of a wide variety of topics: trade and fiscal policies; trends in wages, incomes, and prices; the causes of the productivity slowdown; labor-market problems; rural and urban policies; inflation; state-level economic development strategies; comparative international economic performance; and studies of the overall health of the U.S. manufacturing sector and of specific key industries.

The Institute works with a growing network of innovative economists and other social science researchers in universities and research centers all over the country who are willing to go beyond the conventional wisdom in considering strategies for public policy.

Founding scholars of the Institute include Jeff Faux, EPI president; Lester Thurow, Sloan School of Management, MIT; Ray Marshall, former U.S. secretary of labor, professor at the LBJ School of Public Affairs, University of Texas; Barry Bluestone, University of Massachusetts-Boston; Robert Reich, former U.S. secretary of labor; and Robert Kuttner, author, editor of *The American Prospect,* and columnist for *Business Week* and the Washington Post Writers Group.

For additional information about the Institute, contact EPI at 1660 L Street, NW, Suite 1200, Washington, DC 20036, (202) 775-8810.